GONE AM I,
CAUGHT BY THE UNDERWORLD,
YET CLEANSED AND ALIVE
IN THE BEYOND....

— From an Old Kingdom funerary text

"We usually think of time as a river, a river like the Nile, with a strong, swift current bearing us further and further away from what we have been and towards the time when we will not be at all — birth, death and the brief transit of life in between. But perhaps we should think of time as a deep, still pool rather than a fast-flowing river. If time were a pool, we could kneel at its edge and gaze at our reflections and then beyond them to what lay deeper still. Instead of looking back at time, we could look down into it — we could peel back the layers of the palimpsest — and now and again different features of the past — different sights and sounds and voices and dreams — would rise to the surface: rise and subside, and the deep pool would hold them all, so that nothing was lost and nothing ever went away."

— Katherine Frank,
Prologue to *Lucie Duff Gordon: A Passage to Egypt,* 1994

CONVERSATIONS WITH
MUMMIES

NEW LIGHT ON THE
LIVES OF ANCIENT EGYPTIANS

BY ROSALIE DAVID AND RICK ARCHBOLD
ADDITIONAL HISTORICAL CONSULTATION BY PETER BRAND

BLACK WALNUT

A BLACK WALNUT BOOK

This edition published in 2007 by
Black Walnut Books, an imprint of
Madison Press Books.

ISBN-13: 978-1-897330-29-6
ISBN-10: 1-897330-29-4

For more information, please contact

Madison Press Books
1000 Yonge Street, Suite 200
Toronto, Ontario
Canada M4W 2K2

Printed in China

A note about the dates: The non-denominational system of time division used in this book, B.C.E. (before the Common Era) and C.E. (Common Era), corresponds to the older system B.C. (before Christ) and A.D. (*anno Domini*).

This book is dedicated to all researchers, past and present, whose contribution to paleopathology continues to advance our understanding of the ancient Egyptians.

CONTENTS

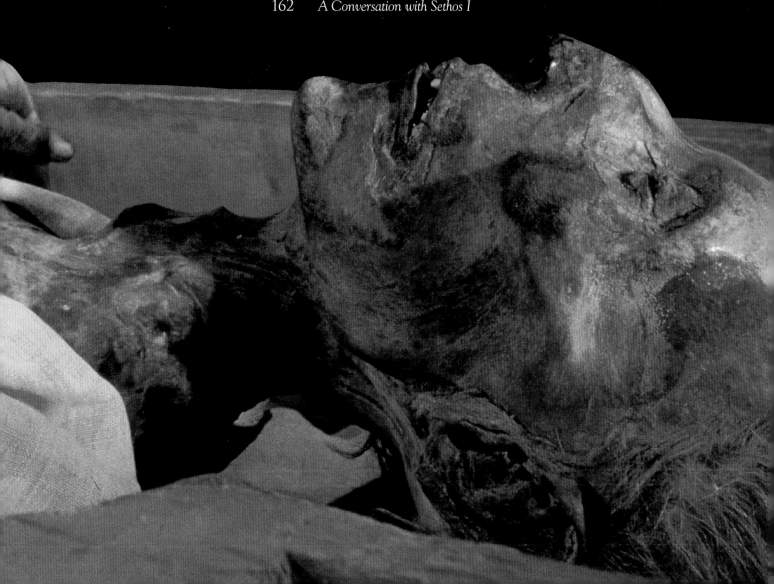

PREFACE

URING MY FIRST VISIT TO EGYPT BACK IN THE LATE 1960s, WHEN I WAS STILL AN UNDERGRADUATE, I naturally made a pilgrimage to the Cairo Museum, the world's greatest storehouse of artifacts from the ancient Egyptian world. The museum offers treasures ranging from the tomb of Tutankhamen and the royal burials of the 21st and 22nd dynasties at Tanis, right through to objects from the most ancient period, such as the Narmer Palette, which commemorates the founding of the Egyptian state in about 3100 B.C.E. But I will admit to a slight feeling of disappointment when I entered the museum's Royal Mummy Room, where the remains of all the pharaohs so far discovered were on display. These potentates lay prone in wooden boxes and were frustratingly difficult to see.

What a difference a little more than 30 years has made. Now the royal mummies are displayed inside well-lit glass cases that allow the visitor to look them in the eye and contemplate the force of character it took to rule as both gods and men. And what a contrast there is in the way we study ancient Egypt a quarter-century later. In the early 1970s, Egyptology was a discipline still closely tied to its 19th-century roots in archeology and anthropology. Now, as a new century dawns, it is an enterprise that ranges from excavating ancient sites to analyzing the DNA of ancient bones. Unquestionably, the most exciting new area of study is the field of paleopathology, which has brought the most sophisticated techniques of medical and biological science to bear on the study of ancient Egyptian mummies.

As the instigator of the Manchester Mummy Project, I've been privileged to play a direct role in this stimulating area of my profession. I must confess, however, that until I started work on *Conversations with Mummies*, I hadn't realized just how rich and fascinating a story I was part of. It is one that will take you from museum storage rooms into modern laboratories, where scientists are daily making exciting discoveries. Working on this book with Rick Archbold has given me a marvelous mountaintop view of the rapidly evolving world of mummy science. I only hope our dialogue with these remarkable people from the distant past will bring the ancient Egyptians and the world they lived in back to life. But as you will shortly discover, our conversations with mummies have only just begun.

Rosalie David, Manchester, England, Spring 2000

PROLOGUE

ROSALIE DAVID LED THE WAY THROUGH A LABYRINTH OF CORRIDORS, IN AND OUT OF CREAKY VICTORIAN buildings, beyond doors that had to be unlocked with a ring of heavy old-fashioned keys. As she passed through one venerable laboratory, she nodded a greeting to the young woman studying what looked like dinosaur bones on a large lab table. As she left the room, Rosalie commented in her soft voice with its gentle echo of her Welsh origins, "That's where they invented the first computer. Manchester can be a surprising place." Finally, in a darkened hallway, she stopped before a door shut with a large padlock.

"The Mummy Store," she announced.

The door swung open, and she led her guest into a warm dry musty space suddenly filled with fluorescent light. At first glance, the room seemed to be like an ordinary storage room, crowded with shelves that rose toward the ceiling, some of their contents swaddled in plastic bubble wrap, the kind used for packing electronic parts and stereo components.

"Would you like to meet Asru?" Rosalie asked. "She had just about every disease imaginable — a wonderful subject for our study."

She rolled a gurney bearing a long wrapped shape into the light, then almost casually lifted back the top layer of bubble wrap. An ancient sunken face, its mouth upturned in a lopsided grin, leered up at us. The body's withered arms were neatly placed upon the pelvis and its emaciated ribcage brought to mind images of famine. The empty eye sockets gaped, unseeing. Then a delicious scent filled the air — spicy, exotic, yet vaguely familiar.

"What's that smell?" the guest asked.

"Why, that's Asru," Rosalie replied. "She was wrapped with spices — possibly myrrh and frankincense, just like in the Bible, and several others. It was a common practice. And the embalmers never used exactly the same combination twice. In fact, almost every mummy has a unique scent. It's quite extraordinary, really, when you think about it. Asru was a temple musician who had probably died during the 25th Dynasty — around 700 B.C.E. — which means the spices you're smelling are nearly three thousand years old. And we have mummies here that are even older, yet the smell is still there. Every mummy is quite unique. After a while one begins to feel as though one knows each of them personally."

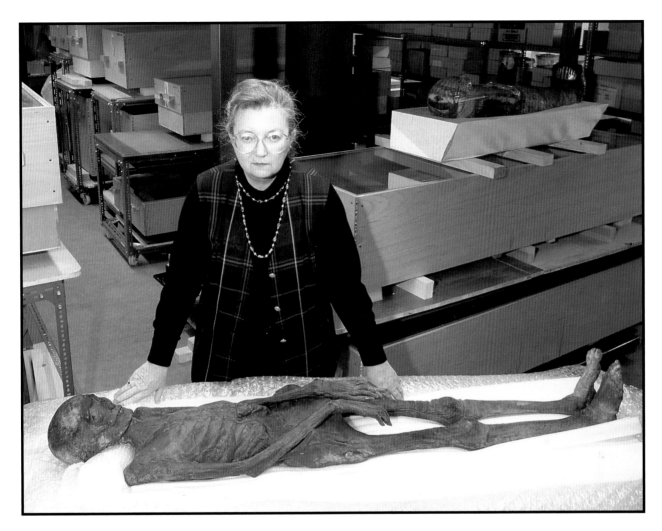

(Above) In the Mummy Store of the Manchester Museum, Rosalie David stands with
the remains of Asru, a member of the museum's impressive mummy collection.
(Below) The Victorian Gothic façade of the Manchester Museum as it appears today.

MANCHESTER SEEMS AN UNLIKELY PLACE FOR ONE OF THE FINEST COLLECTIONS OF ANCIENT Egyptian mummies outside Egypt — 24 in all, not including the animal mummies — until you know a little about the city's history. During the Industrial Revolution, it was a thriving textile center, whose cotton fabrics helped clothe the people of the British Empire. Among the men who made their fortunes from colonial cotton and human toil was Jesse Haworth, a prominent Manchester mill owner during the second half of the 19th century. Once he'd made his fortune, Haworth began to wonder what he was going to do with it.

Like many Victorian men of affairs, Haworth was a devout Christian in an age when modern science, and notably the theories of Charles Darwin, was challenging ancient verities. But one realm of scientific endeavor promised to confirm the Bible's teaching rather than undermine it: the emerging discipline of Egyptology. The Book of Exodus tells perhaps the most famous story of the Old Testament, that of the exile of the Jews in Egypt during the time of the pharaohs and their long trek through the desert to the Promised Land. Surely the men who were digging up the tombs and cities of ancient Egypt would unearth some of the places mentioned in the Bible? Maybe one of them would discover a remnant of the exile in Egypt or evidence of Moses' long march home.

When Haworth decided to contribute part of his accumulated wealth to this high-minded quest, he chose to back the expeditions of Flinders Petrie, a young archeologist who would come to be regarded as the founder of scientific Egyptology and was later knighted for his work. It was Petrie, for example, who looked beyond the pyramids and other great monuments to investigate such seemingly insignificant artifacts as pottery shards, which earlier excavators had simply tossed away. He was one of the first to attempt to identify Egyptian pottery by period and then to use this knowledge to accurately date a site.

As a result of Petrie's excavations, Jesse Haworth found himself in possession of a major collection of Egyptian artifacts of everyday life. To house this collection, he built an extension to the Manchester Museum — a glorious Victorian Gothic edifice on the fringe of central Manchester — which had become part of the university in 1888. The first Keeper of Egyptology at the Manchester Museum was a young disciple of Petrie named Margaret Murray, who performed an early mummy autopsy. The current holder of the post is Dr. Rosalie David.

In the nearly one hundred years that now separate these two remarkable women, the study of ancient Egypt has evolved into a sophisticated, multidisciplinary enterprise combining history, science, linguistics, and anthropology. Of all the advances being made, some of the most exciting have come by way of medical analysis of ancient Egyptian mummies. A world leader in this field is the Manchester Museum, home of the Manchester Mummy Project. The Mummy Project is Rosalie David's brainchild.

ROSALIE GENTLY REPOSITIONED THE BUBBLE WRAP OVER THE SLEEPING ASRU, THEN INTRODUCED several more of the Manchester mummies as if they were old friends. Here was the child known only as No. 1770, on whom Dr. David and a group of colleagues from the university's Medical School had performed one of the world's first modern mummy autopsies, in June of 1975. And here was a female figure ordinarily identified as No. 1766, but currently nicknamed the Test Case Mummy. In a laboratory in the Medical School across the road from the Mummy Store,

Among the treasures of the Manchester Museum's collection are mummies dating from almost every era in Egyptian history, including the New Kingdom (far left) and the Greco-Roman Period (middle left and right), when portrait masks depicting the deceased (far right) became popular.

tiny fragments of the Test Case Mummy's body were being used to develop repeatable techniques for performing disease studies on ancient tissue.

In a sense, Rosalie David and her eclectic group of investigators resembled nothing so much as a team of police detectives and forensic scientists investigating a suspected homicide. If the culprit, in this case an ancient disease or diseases, happened to be more than two thousand years old, that only made the detective work more difficult and more exciting. And if the scene of the crime could only be imagined, at least they had the body.

Despite its tomblike nature, the Mummy Store did not have a ghoulish atmosphere. It seemed, rather, to be a peaceful and contemplative place, a place where age-old questions were asking to be answered. If the spirits of these ancient Egyptians had long departed, their individual lives begged for the immortality of our understanding.

Rosalie shut off the lights, closed the door, and locked the padlock with a quiet click. But as she threaded the way back through the labyrinth toward the bustle of late-20th-century Manchester, the scent of Asru seemed to linger — spicy and exotic, yet somehow familiar.

CHAPTER ONE

THE MUMMY PROJECT

O N THE MORNING OF JUNE 10, 1975, THE OPERATING THEATER AT THE MANCHESTER University Medical School looked like the set for a live taping of a hospital drama — complete with packed studio audience. The spectators, actually a distinguished group that included the Lord Mayor of Manchester and many members of the university elite, fell silent as the cast — a team of figures wearing green surgical gowns and masks — took the stage. Two of these figures, a man and a woman, stepped forward, toward the diminutive cadaver that lay on the operating table. One of the two, a young woman whose long hair was tied in a bun, began to snip through the strange bandages wrapped around the body. A television camera zoomed in to get a close-up of her gloved hands.

What was 29-year-old Dr. Rosalie David thinking as she carefully cut her way through the outer wrappings of Mummy 1770? She seemed oblivious to the BBC television cameras that followed her every move, to the arc lights that illuminated this strange scene as brightly as an Egyptian midday sun. Perhaps she was reminding herself that with each snip of the surgical scissors, she was cutting through some two thousand years of history.

Three years of planning and preparation — not to mention the discoveries of a century and a half of Egyptology — had led to this moment, Britain's first modern autopsy of an Egyptian mummy. Recent advances in medical technology and methods of analysis promised that this would be an autopsy like none other in forensic history. But just what could this team of experts hope to discover about the human being buried inside these ancient bandages? What light could modern science shed on one ancient life? On life in ancient times?

The mummy on the dissecting table presented plenty of puzzles beyond the

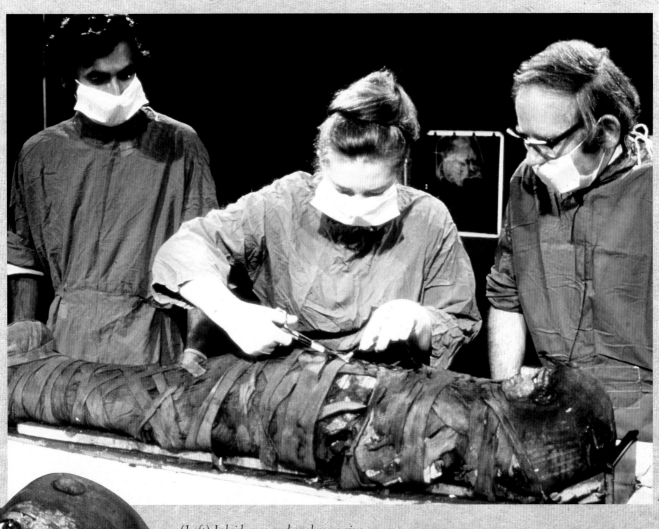

(Left) Inlaid eyes and eyebrows give Mummy 1770's cartonnage mask a haunting doll-like appearance. (Above) Dr. Rosalie David makes the first incision, while her colleagues Dr. Edmund Tapp (on the right) and Dr. Ali Ahmed look on. (Right) Dr. David and the investigative team with Mummy 1770 before the autopsy.

mystery of its name. Where, for example, had it come from? Mummy 1770 was believed to have been discovered by pioneering Egyptologist Sir Flinders Petrie during an excavation at Hawara in 1910-11, but this belief was based on indirect references in Petrie's diary and in one of his letters. It was also not clear how long ago this person had lived. The simple head cover made of carton-nage — a sort of papier mâché using papyrus or linen mixed with gum — suggested a date during the early Greco-Roman period, when Egypt was ruled by the Ptolemies, who had inherited the country from Alexander the Great.

X-rays of the mummy taken before the unwrapping had done little to clarify the mystery. Within the layers of bandages lay a child of indeter-minate sex, probably a teenager at the time of death. (Because human bones pass through clearly marked stages as they grow, it is easier to deter-mine the age of the skeleton of a still-growing adolescent than of a fully mature adult.) The lower limbs were missing, but the manner of their amputation was unclear. And close to the ends of the leg bones, the X-rays showed a rounded object that gave rise to all sorts of speculation in the press, including the theory that this was the body of a newborn child. Was this a very young mother buried with her baby, both of them having died in the process of birth?

(Above) Beneath the mask, Mummy 1770's facial and upper jaw bones were covered with a layer of mud and bandage fragments. (Opposite) A careful cleaning revealed a defect in the bone on the left side of the nose that could have caused chronic nasal congestion.

In the wrappings around the right leg, a human canine tooth was vis-ible. This tiny clue, combined with the jumbled nature of the ribs and the collapsed area on the right side of the skull, suggested but did not prove that the mummy had been interfered with at some stage after burial, prob-ably by tomb robbers, then subsequently rewrapped. The X-rays also showed up three dense spots in the abdomen.

"What have we here?"

The query came from Dr. Edmund Tapp, co-leader of the autopsy team. With a pair of tweezers, he delicately extracted a tiny object from within the wrappings and held it up to the light. The TV cameras dollied forward to get a closer look at this first "discovery." Their lenses magnified the body of an ancient beetle — one of many insects that had lived and died within the mummy's bandages. Dr. Tapp, then a senior consulting pathologist at Manchester's Withington Hospital, placed the beetle in a specimen box, which was immediately labeled by one of the other gowned figures. He'd performed thousands of autopsies in his day, but never one like this.

Under the unrelenting arc lights, the room grew hotter as the morning wore on. But the Egyptologist and the pathologist kept working, delicately removing each morsel of bandage. Occasionally, the BBC director for the *Chronicle* series interrupted with a request for a bit of staged conversation to help explain what was happening. Otherwise, they worked mostly in silence before a rapt audience.

The bandages, like everything found with or within the body, would subsequently be analyzed by one of the members of an impressive team of scientists and archeologists. It was therefore essential that nothing be contaminated with the dust or microbes of the 20th century — hence, the surgical masks and gloves, which were used to protect the mummy more than the wearers.

The team was conducting the unwrapping like an archeological excavation, layer by layer, carefully labeling each item discovered and noting its context. Beneath the outermost wrappings, the bandages became pieces of much wider material, an indication that the embalmers had cut some corners. Once the last bandages had been removed from the neck, the team was ready to tackle the delicate task of removing the mummy's cartonnage head cover, which had been painted in standard Ptolemaic style, a generic portrait of indeterminate gender. The main portion of the mask had broken away from its base, exposing fragments of shattered skull.

Dr. Tapp cautiously lifted away the loose bone fragments, anxious to avoid inflicting fresh damage. Then he and Rosalie pulled away the intact portion of the mask, exposing what was left of the cranium. The upper jaw and face area were still of a piece. Rosalie swept the skull clean with a tiny brush, just as she would have done with a shard of pottery unearthed during an archeological dig. She could see the tiny aperture in the bone at the end of the nasal passage, through which the embalmers had removed the brain, a procedure now imitated in certain types of brain surgery. The cranial bones showed traces of the red and blue paint sometimes applied during mummification, a sign that little if any flesh had remained on the skull at the time of embalming. Curious.

19

The autopsy team moved on to the torso, removing a large square bandage to reveal a cartonnage breast cover brightly colored in hues of pink, yellow, and black. It came away in one piece. When the last bandages were peeled back from the upper torso, the mummy was revealed to be resting with crossed arms, a position that deliberately mimicked the classic pose of Osiris, Egyptian god of the afterlife. Only traces of flesh remained on the mummy's arms, all of it dry and easily crumbled. Here the work became especially difficult and time consuming, as the team used tweezers to remove each tiny fragment of parchment skin or powdery flesh.

The first real surprise of the autopsy came as Dr. David and Dr. Tapp commenced their careful unwrapping of the hands. Originally, each digit had been wound separately, though much of the bandaging had come away. Patient unwinding of one of the still-wrapped fingers was soon rewarded with a wonderful discovery: a gold finger stall, or nail cover. Within the loose wrappings, other gold nail covers were found, ten in all, along with fragments of gold leaf. And the loose wrappings of the upper abdomen gave up the greatest prize: two gold nipple covers. Apparently, the deceased child was female.

As was often the case for a mummy from the Greco-Roman period (332 B.C.E.-ca. 600 C.E.), the team found no packages of internal organs inside the abdominal cavity. The practice of including these canopic packages inside the embalmed body had gradually died out as the art of mummification evolved following the Hellenistic conquest of Egypt. One of the three dense spots seen on the X-rays — this one in the abdominal wall — turned out to be a nodule consisting of the calcified remains of a Guinea worm, a common parasite in the ancient Middle East. (The nipple covers accounted for the other two spots.) The body cavity had been packed with a combination of mud and bandages, in an effort to preserve the body's shape.

But what was this? A small roll of bandages extended from the wrappings below the ruined pelvic area. From its shape and position, it could have only one purpose: to represent a missing phallus. Here was a real mystery, a mummy at one moment female, at the next male. Had the sex of the child been uncertain? If so, why?

As Rosalie and her colleagues unwrapped the legs, they added more details to the confusing picture. The shorter, right leg had been artificially lengthened — with a wooden limb splinted to the femur — and covered with mud during the mummification process, to make it as long as what remained of the left leg. The round object that had caused so much speculation proved to be two artificial feet, shod with beautifully decorated slippers and adorned with gilded toenail covers. So much for the notion that this was the body of a young mother with her child, perhaps mutilated and killed because she had borne her baby out of wedlock.

20

As the autopsy progressed, Rosalie David and her colleagues uncovered tantalizing clues about Mummy 1770's identity: gold finger stalls (above), generally reserved for the upper classes; artificial feet shod with a magnificent pair of decorated cartonnage slippers (right); and prosthetic legs carefully attached to the bones of the amputated limbs (below), so that the mummy would appear whole (bottom).

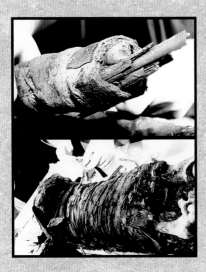

Given the care taken and the presence of gold ornaments, there seemed little question the embalmers had regarded this mutilated child as a person of some importance. If the autopsy team had found few clues as to the child's identity, they nonetheless had reason to be elated. No one had expected so many interesting discoveries or such a fascinating puzzle.

The foregoing account compresses two solid weeks of slow meticulous work, day after day, under the glare of the lights before a hushed audience that evolved from a crowd of prominent guests on the first day into an audience of the truly interested and informed — including most of Rosalie's students at the university. But Rosalie remembers no sense of drudgery. She felt the same sort of energy that seizes field archeologists when they strike the first evidence of a real find. And like archeologists in the field, the "excavation" of Mummy 1770 was only the first step in understanding the world from which it came.

AS ROSALIE DAVID PERFORMED THE 1975 AUTOPSY OF MUMMY 1770, SHE WAS ACUTELY conscious of the woman who had led the way many years before. In 1908, at the University of Manchester, Margaret Murray had unwrapped the mummies of two brothers found in an intact 12th Dynasty, or Middle Kingdom, tomb (1991-1786 B.C.E.). The Tomb of the Two Brothers, the finest intact non-royal tomb group ever found from that era, is still the jewel of the Manchester Museum's Egyptian collection.

When Rosalie began thinking about performing her own mummy autopsy, she studied the book written by her pioneering predecessor, one of the first women to make a mark as an Egyptologist. In many ways, Murray's double autopsy was an inspiration for Rosalie's work. In 1908, she had brought together a group of outside specialists, a team of experts in disciplines ranging from biochemistry to archeology, who had analyzed the wrappings and human remains with all the science at their disposal. But in the nearly 70 years that had passed since then, no similar autopsy had been performed on British soil.

The idea for the Mummy Project had occurred to Rosalie David soon after she arrived as a young Egyptologist at the Manchester Museum in 1972. Just before she took up her post, all the human mummies then in the museum collection had been X-rayed by a portable machine, a most unsatisfactory situation. "If we're going to do this sort of thing," Rosalie said to herself, "then let's do it properly." She suggested the idea to her superiors and let it waft across the campus and into town. Soon volunteers began offering their services. The museum promised to provide financial support. Before she knew it, Rosalie was organizing a team that was planning its first autopsy.

As Rosalie first formulated it, the Mummy Project had two aims: (1) to look for evidence of disease and the causes of death in Egyptian mummies while gaining further information about life and death in ancient Egypt and (2) to come up with a standard method for examining ancient remains that could be used by Egyptologists and other students of ancient cultures around the world.

The Mummy Project was about combining modern scientific knowledge with the latest developments in Egyptology in order to learn more about how the Egyptians lived and died. Such an

Dr. Margaret Murray (second from right), first curator of the Manchester Museum's extensive Egyptian collection, was a pioneer in the field of multidisciplinary mummy studies. Her 1908 autopsy of the Two Brothers brought together experts from such fields as anatomy, chemistry, and textile studies.

enterprise represented an important forward step for a venerable but newly energized scholarly discipline, the field of paleopathology — literally, the study of ancient disease. To study a human disease, you need human bodies; to study an ancient disease, you need ancient bodies. The thousands of Egyptian mummies preserved in museums and private collections around the world and the many thousands more that still lie buried beneath the desert sand were all potential subjects for the Mummy Project. When reduced to its essence, paleopathology is just another way of saying "mummy science."

LIKE INVESTIGATORS AT THE SCENE OF AN ANCIENT CRIME, THE MUMMY PROJECT TEAM had gathered the evidence over the course of those two arduous and exciting weeks in Manchester in June 1975. Some of it was contradictory, which led to all sorts of speculation, some of it far-fetched. When the first gold ornaments were discovered, for instance, the more sensational newspaper reports had immediately announced that Mummy 1770 was an ancient Egyptian princess. But such conclusions were a long way off for the investigators. First the discoveries needed to be sifted and analyzed for every available clue. Only then could sound hypotheses be put forward.

The autopsy of Mummy 1770 presented several very specific questions, the most obvious one being: Was the child a male or a female? The pelvic area had been too badly damaged to settle this question, but careful measurement of the skull could offer clues. (The proportions of a male skull are measurably different from those of a female skull.) When the measurements were taken, it became clear that the body had belonged to a female. But most of the remaining questions were neither so easily nor so conclusively answered.

QUESTION ONE:
Had the head and rib bones been broken and the legs amputated before or after death?

To answer this question, the investigators looked for callus, the regenerative tissue formed by a broken bone that is quite different in appearance from the original bone. Although they found no callus anywhere on the skeleton, this did not rule out a fracture, since it takes some time for callus to form. If, for example, the child had died shortly after her legs had been cut off, the callus would not have had time to develop.

The tentative conclusion? Of the broken bones, only the amputated limbs seemed likely to have been broken just before the child's death, and these fractures were quite possibly the result of the event that caused the death. Perhaps the girl had been killed by falling masonry that crushed the lower parts of her legs. Or maybe she had drowned in the Nile and been partly eaten by a hippo or a crocodile. Or perhaps the legs were amputated because they had become ulcerous due to Guinea worm infestation.

QUESTION TWO:
What can explain the presence of both the nipple shields and the artificial phallus?

The body may have been embalmed in an advanced state of decomposition, making the sex uncertain. So by including both the nipple shields and the phallus, the embalmers might have been hedging their bets. This still does not explain why the body came to be left so long to decay — if that is what actually happened.

QUESTION THREE:

How long had the body putrefied before being mummified?

The almost complete absence of soft tissue on the mummy's skeleton caused the team to speculate that the body had been decaying for a considerable time before being mummified. The blue and red paint visible on the skull and the fact that the bandages near the amputation points of the legs adhered directly to the bone seemed strong evidence of a corpse in an advanced state of decomposition. This decay might have been deliberate, since the ancient Egyptians sometimes allowed female corpses to putrefy so as to discourage necrophilia. But Rosalie argued it was unlikely that any body would have been allowed to decay this far. Another possibility was that the body had spent days or even weeks in water. Perhaps the girl had drowned and then been partly eaten.

QUESTION FOUR:

How had Mummy 1770 died?

The crocodile theory appealed to many, since the crocodile was an animal held sacred by the ancient Egyptians, which might account for the respect paid to the body — and certainly a crocodile might attack a child in the water. Unfortunately for this theory, however, a crocodile does not ordinarily bite through bone, preferring to grab a limb and shake it until it separates at the joint.

The Guinea worm found in the abdominal wall would not in itself have killed the girl, but it undoubtedly sapped the strength of this unlucky teenager and may explain her missing legs.

QUESTION FIVE:

*Could any of the evidence from the unwrapping bring us any closer to figuring out
exactly who this person was and when and how she had lived?*

The gold ornaments suggested a person of wealth and rank. (The damage to the mummy's mask seemed clear evidence that tomb robbers had removed other valuable ornaments gracing the neck and head.) But beyond this very general hypothesis, little could be ventured. The autopsy had yielded only the ghost of a clue as to Mummy 1770's identity.

THE FACE OF 1770

More than thirty fragments of bone were painstakingly cleaned, cast in plastic, and reassembled to form a model of 1770's skull. Using this model — and some educated guesswork — the Manchester forensic team was able to recreate the rounded, adolescent features of Mummy 1770 (left). A bone defect which could have caused nasal congestion explains why the model's mouth was left slightly open: blocked nasal passages might have forced her to breathe through her mouth.

But exactly who was Mummy 1770? The evidence is frustratingly vague. Perhaps she was the daughter of a court official or nobleman. And just what was it that convinced the priests who ornamented her damaged body that she warranted such a fine reburial? Presumably her remains were discovered in a plundered tomb. Either from the importance of the tomb or the quality of the grave goods, these later Egyptians concluded that this mystery girl was someone important.

(Right) A Guinea worm. The larva of this parasite enters the body in drinking water. Eventually, it may grow into a three-foot-long adult  *worm that exits the body through painful burning blisters in the lower legs. Perhaps these crippling sores prompted the amputation of 1770's legs.*

As for just when the girl had died, dating her bones and bandages promised to be a simpler matter. Radiocarbon (Carbon-14) analysis of both bone and linen samples was performed in the Chemistry Department of the University of Manchester. The results from this analysis were later confirmed by scientists elsewhere — and they were surprising, to say the least.

The bones of Mummy 1770 were more than a thousand years older than the bandages that wrapped them. The bones were dated at ca. 1000 B.C.E.; the linen at ca. 380 C.E. (Radiocarbon dating is generally considered accurate to within plus or minus 150 years.) This child had not died two hundred years after the birth of Christ, when Egypt was part of the Roman Empire. She had possibly lived during the 21st Dynasty. Mummy 1770 had died more than three thousand years ago.

With this revelation, the autopsy evidence suddenly looked very different. If the mummy had been rewrapped more than a thousand years after its initial burial, the rewrappers were probably priests who believed the body represented an important personage, possibly even someone of royal blood, but someone of uncertain sex. It was they who had added the false limbs and the false feet and had decorated the body with gold ornaments.

Rewrapping also provided a completely new explanation for the absence of soft tissue on the skeleton, which would have adhered to the original bandages and come away with them when the mummy was unwrapped. The fact of rewrapping did not eliminate the various theories about how the child had died and how long the body had decayed before its original mummification, but it made them less persuasive.

The Carbon-14 dating both clarified and deepened the mystery. As so often in Egyptology, the researchers were left with as many questions as answers.

ROSALIE DAVID STARTED ASKING QUESTIONS ABOUT ANCIENT EGYPT WHEN SHE WAS SIX YEARS OLD. One day at school she was shown a book with a line drawing of three pyramids. She knows now that this was an early-20th-century German reconstruction drawing of the pyramids at Abusir, drawn as the German archeologist imagined they would have looked in ancient times with their great causeways sloping down to the Nile. But the six-year-old Rosalie only knew they were pictures of something very old.

"The moment I saw the drawing of those pyramids, I knew I wanted to be an Egyptologist," she says now. "I probably didn't even know the word *Egyptologist* then, but I knew I wanted to spend my life studying ancient Egypt. What a strange notion for a six-year-old girl to have! Yet if you talk to other Egyptologists, many of them will tell you of a similar childhood experience. In my case, it was a visual thing, something about the shape of the pyramids made a huge impact on me. I can't explain it. The drawings themselves are quite ordinary. I really haven't a clue why they triggered my young imagination so profoundly."

When she got home from school that afternoon, she announced to her parents that she wanted to become an Egyptologist. They nodded kindly and assumed this silly notion would go away.

To her parents' surprise, Rosalie's childhood fascination with Egyptology only deepened over time. She chose her secondary school courses with an eye to her future career, studying Greek and Latin, history and geography, and she continued to read voraciously about Egypt and archeology.

"As soon as my parents would let me — I think I was eleven — I went on local archeological digs around Cardiff, Wales, where I grew up. During school holidays, I would join excavations organized by Cardiff University. I believe I was the youngest schoolchild they had ever had. We excavated both Mesolithic and Roman sites. I loved it, even though I only got to do the menial work. But it taught me that I didn't mind the kind of painstaking detail that is a feature of all good archeology. The whole time, however, I never lost my fascination with Egypt. British archeology was interesting, but it wasn't my life's work."

In 1964, after passing her A levels, she was accepted to University College London, which offered a degree in Ancient History, with Egypt as its main focus. She was the only student in that group who planned to become an Egyptologist.

Rosalie David, at left, arrives in Luxor with camera and references close to hand on her first trip to Egypt in 1966, as part of a Dutch tour group.

At University College in those days, every student in Ancient History who passed the first-year exams was given a grant from a fund left by an anonymous American donor. The only condition to the grant was that it be spent on a trip to Greece, Italy, or Egypt. Rosalie couldn't believe her good fortune — she had been saving money toward a trip to Egypt for many years.

"As much as I had read about Egypt and as hard as I had studied, nothing quite prepared me for that first trip there in the spring of 1966. I was just 19, so it was quite an adventure.

"I remember being afraid that the real Egypt would be a major letdown after all the years I'd spent dreaming of going there, but if anything, the experience exceeded my expectations. Cairo had not yet suffered the population explosion and urban decay that would destroy so many of its charms. I remember especially the beautiful gardens going down to the Nile. They're all gone now.

"We followed the usual tourist itinerary — Cairo, the pyramids, Luxor, the Valley of the Kings — so I saw, essentially, the Egypt that tourists see. But it didn't matter. Here were the great monuments that I'd studied, that I'd seen in pictures — but in their real place, a place that in many ways hadn't changed for thousands of years. I found the whole experience quite overwhelming.

"But then who hasn't been overwhelmed by the Pyramids of Giza? They have been aweing tourists for millennia and I was no exception. Of course, our tour itinerary included a visit to the pyramids at night for the famous "*Son et Lumière*" — one of the oldest sound and light shows on the planet. I remember sitting there with my feet in the sand of Egypt and watching the lights come up on the Great Pyramid of Cheops and thinking to myself, "I'm here, I'm really here!" It seemed unbelievable. So, no, my first trip to Egypt was anything but a disappointment."

Rosalie didn't return to Egypt until the second year of her Ph.D. program at the University of Liverpool, by which time she was hard at work on her dissertation about how the temple worked as a ritual unit in ancient Egypt. Her study focused on the most beautiful temple in Egypt, that of King Sethos I (1318-1304 B.C.E.) at Abydos, a Mecca of the ancient Egyptian world, which was connected to the cult of the risen god Osiris. In Liverpool, she had translated its superbly preserved interior inscriptions from photographs. Now she would be able to check her translations against the originals.

She spent six weeks at Abydos, working alone by day but staying at an excavation house out in the desert with a group of American archeologists from the University of Pennsylvania who were working on early dynastic tombs in the area. Early each morning, the Americans drove her by Land Rover to the temple and left her there. Then they would pick her up before sunset.

"Abydos in those days was very much off the tourist route," she remembers. "It was quite remote. Yet I thought nothing about spending the whole day there alone with no one around except the temple guardians. I don't remember being in any sense frightened, alone in this great empty temple built sometime around 1300 B.C.E.

"Actually, there was one other daily visitor, an eccentric Englishwoman who lived in the nearby village, who believed she was the reincarnation of a temple priestess. Her English name was Dorothy Eady, but the locals called her Omm Seti, which means 'mother of Seti,' because she had named her son after the pharaoh. She had lived in the village for 40 years and was quite eccentric. She performed the ancient rituals daily. But she was actually quite knowledgeable about the temple and the old rituals, so we got on pretty well. I treated her with the proper respect."

In ancient times, pilgrims traveled to the temple of King Sethos I at Abydos to pay homage to the god Osiris, master of the afterlife, to whom the temple is dedicated. But unless these pilgrims were very important indeed, they would never have entered the temple itself. During one of the great festivals, however, they might have been permitted as far as the colossal outer hypostyle hall (opposite), as grand today as it was in ancient times. No ordinary Egyptian ever saw the magnificent Gallery of the Kings (above) where King Sethos listed the name of every pharaoh dating back to Menes, who unified Egypt.

(Top) These stones are all that remains of the Osirean of Sethos I, what is possibly a false tomb built by the pharaoh behind the great temple. Though Sethos himself was not buried here, the tomb was constructed to provide the ruler with a monumental connection to Osiris in this world and the next.

Rosalie David's Ph.D. thesis would become the basis for her first book, *Religious Ritual at Abydos*, but on graduation she faced a more immediate problem than getting published: finding a job in her chosen field. Then, as now, a Ph.D. in Egyptology meant an almost certain guarantee of unemployment (though, today, many graduates in Egyptology are hired by computer firms; it seems that if you can decipher hieroglyphs, writing software is a breeze). But Rosalie was more determined than most. Her *alma mater*, University College, created a temporary post for her — mundane cataloguing at the Petrie Museum, which housed the personal collection of Sir Flinders Petrie. The pay was low, but it was enough to get by.

Nine months later, in the spring of 1972, she learned that the Manchester Museum was looking for an Egyptologist. Rosalie applied and went up to Manchester for her interview, a two-and-a-half-hour train ride north of London. She remembers walking through the museum's Egyptian galleries with growing wonder. Here was the other half of Flinders Petrie's personal collection, one of the world's best assemblages of objects from ancient everyday life, yet for years it had not been promoted and was not widely known.

She got the job, no doubt partly because of her connection with the Petrie Museum in London. Three years later she was on national television conducting a mummy autopsy. She was on the cover of *Newsweek*. It was all a bit overwhelming for the shy young woman from Cardiff.

THE ROSETTA STONE: BREAKING THE EGYPTIAN CODE

When Napoleon's troops uncovered this black basalt slab (right) near the town of Rosetta, they had no idea its inscriptions held the key to an ancient mystery. The Rosetta Stone, as it has come to be called, dated from 196 B.C.E. and was inscribed in two languages, ancient Greek and ancient Egyptian, but in three scripts: Greek, hieroglyphs, and Demotic, a cursive version of hieroglyphs that had gradually replaced the more cumbersome hieroglyphic script as the alphabet in everyday use. When scholars examined the stone, they were able to read the ancient Greek, which proved to be a decree passed on the first anniversary of the coronation of Ptolemy V. It seemed clear that the same text had been written in the three scripts, but after several years, only a few fragments of the Demotic had been deciphered.

Copies of the stone's inscriptions lay on the desks of four European scholars: two Frenchmen, one Swede, and one Englishman. Each wanted to be the first to decipher the Rosetta Stone. But even after 20 years, they were little closer to a solution. Finally, in 1822, Jean-François Champollion made the breakthrough that had eluded the others, concluding that the ancient Egyptian language was a combination of both ideographic and phonetic script. The French had won the race, but it would take many more years of hard scholarly labor before Egyptologists would be able to read hieroglyphs with any ease.

(Above) The Rosetta Stone, key to a modern understanding of hieroglyphs. (Left) Champollion, who deciphered the Rosetta Stone, went on to publish an Egyptian grammar and dictionary. (Opposite) Hieroglyphs were probably comprehensible to less than 5 percent of the ancient population and were used mainly in inscriptions and on monuments. Educated and literate Egyptians used Demotic for most of their correspondence and record keeping.

Rosalie David had realized what other Egyptologists in other parts of the world were also beginning to see. The time was ripe for a true marriage of traditional Egyptology and modern science. The accumulated knowledge of ancient Egypt was great, but the gaps were still enormous. In 1975, a great deal was known about the ancient Egyptians, but what was known paled beside the mysteries as yet unplumbed.

The temples and monuments that Egyptologists had studied since the days of Napoleon were made of stone and so had survived for thousands of years — unlike the houses of the ordinary people. (Their dwellings were built of mud brick and most had long since washed away.) Our knowledge of this ancient people was therefore incomplete, like our understanding of their language.

In the 150 years since the Rosetta Stone (a 2nd-century B.C.E. decree) was deciphered by a French linguist, scholars had learned to read the puzzling symbols the ancient Egyptians inscribed on their great funerary monuments and inside their massive temples. They had translated many of the surviving papyri. But all this labor added up to only a fragmentary understanding of a vast and sophisticated ancient literature. And much of what had been translated was based on guesswork. Many words and phrases, even whole texts, remained obscure for lack of sufficient context.

What did the ancient Egyptian language sound like? Scholars could only guess. Hieroglyphs consist almost entirely of consonants, with no vowels, and the spoken language has long since passed out of use. The only existing descendant of ancient Egyptian is Coptic, which today survives only as the liturgical language of the Christian Coptic Church.

The missing vowels resembled the gaps in modern knowledge of ancient Egypt that faced young Egyptologists like Rosalie David in the 1970s. The Mummy Project, with its first great success, the autopsy of Mummy 1770, was one of several pioneering efforts to bring scientific knowledge to bear on ancient questions.

But after Mummy 1770, what? For practical as well as other reasons, mummy autopsies can't be performed every day. The store of mummified cadavers is limited, and there are religious sensibilities to be considered. Clearly, the next step was to develop a set of non-invasive techniques that could allow paleopathologists to examine an ancient body without unwrapping it and that would begin to fill in those tantalizing lacunae. Mummy science was entering a new and exciting phase of its young history.

A CONVERSATION WITH THE TWO BROTHERS

When I arrived at the Manchester Museum in 1972, I immediately became fascinated by the Two Brothers. The entire contents of their 12th-Dynasty (1991-1786 B.C.E.) tomb-coffins — a canopic chest containing the organs of the younger of the two mummies, and a fascinating array of ritual objects, including beautifully carved boats with rowers — were in a large glass display case in the center of one of the galleries. Within the small world of the museum, they were quite famous, the pride of the collection, but I'd never heard of them before — or heard anything about Margaret Murray's autopsy of them in 1908. All the same, one didn't need to know anything about the Two Brothers to be intrigued. How could these two men, found buried together in an undisturbed tomb from the 12th Dynasty, yet different in so many ways, have been brothers?

When Murray directed the 1908 autopsy of the Two Brothers, she and her colleagues found themselves facing a real puzzle. The inscriptions on the coffins, along with the standard prayers and invocations, identified each as the son of the same mother, Aa-Khnum, sometimes rendered as Khnumu-aa. The inscriptions also designated these brothers as sons of a hatia-prince, the term for a nomarch, or district governor. (As was customary, only the mother's given name is found on the coffins.)

(Left) The reconstructed faces of Khnum-Nakht, at left, and Nekht-Ankh, the occupants of the best-preserved non-royal tomb from the Middle Kingdom. But were they really brothers?

The coffin belonging to the older brother, Khnum-Nakht, also described him as a priest at the temple of Khnumu, but that of the younger brother, Nekht-Ankh, bore no such honorific. Yet, as Flinders Petrie noted at the time the tomb was discovered, "the second coffin and body coffin [belonging to the older brother] are much inferior." Nekht-Ankh's somewhat finer coffin — Petrie exaggerates the differences — was also accompanied by a canopic box, containing four canopic jars, further evidence of a burial that was somewhat more expensive and elaborate.

Even more than the coffins that held them, the two bodies presented a study in contrasts. After unwrapping, Murray noted that the skin on Nekht-Ankh's face was "perfectly preserved," and that "the hair remained on the sides of the face. The hair was dark brown, turning gray, and the length of it on the head was three-quarters of an inch." When the body of the priest Khnum-Nakht was unwrapped, however, "it resolved into a fine powder which rose in clouds when the mummy was handled." Overall, much greater care had been taken to embalm Nekht-Ankh. Whether or not the differences in the coffins and in the quality of embalming indicate a difference in status or are simply historical accidents remains a subject for conjecture.

Dr. John Cameron, the member of the autopsy team who conducted the anatomical examination, discovered far more startling distinctions between the two brothers. His analysis of the skeletons indicated that Nekht-Ankh had died no later than in middle life, while Khnum-Nakht was at least 60 when he had died, a venerable age in ancient Egypt. Yet inscriptions

(Opposite) The coffin of the younger brother, Nekht-Ankh, seen on the right, is the finer of the two. But this may have less to do with the men's differing social status than with economic realities at the time of their burials. (Above) Margaret Murray leads the autopsy of the Two Brothers in 1908. (Right) Among the grave goods were these two miniature boats, meant to provide each brother with transportation up and down the river in the next world.

37

on the linen wrappings indicated that the older brother had died only one year before his much younger brother. While a woman can theoretically bear two sons 30 years apart, such an accomplishment does stretch probability. Even more intriguing, Dr. Cameron concluded that "the appearance represented by the skeleton of Nekht-Ankh is suggestive of its being a eunuch." He based this conclusion on the condition of the genitals and other anatomical features. Recent analysis has yielded no evidence to contradict these findings.

The final and most intriguing piece of this increasingly complex puzzle came from a careful comparison of the skulls, which suggested that the "two brothers" might not have been blood brothers at all, "because of the remarkable racial difference in the features presented by each." The skull of Nekht-Ankh, the younger, "eunuchoid," brother, was of the orthognathous, or non-negroid, type; the skull of the priest was prognathous, or negroid. How could two brothers be so different?

In the more than 90 years since the Two Brothers were unwrapped and examined in Manchester, various theories have been advanced to explain their true relationship. (Modern analysis confirms that they are racially distinct.) Because the inscriptions on their coffins refer to a common mother, Aa-Khnumu, perhaps they were half-brothers, sharing a mother but having racially different fathers. But then how could they both have been sons of the district governor? More likely, given the large difference in their ages, one of them was adopted. Perhaps the adopted son had been born to a concubine in the nomarch's household.

We know little about adoption in ancient Egypt, but it was an established legal procedure. Either a man or a woman could adopt a child simply by writing the child into their will. One of the few documented examples of adoption involves a childless scribe in a village of royal tombmakers who adopted a younger man so as to make him his legal heir. But this motive does not explain the situation of the Two Brothers, and we do not know whether adoption was rare or common.

From the evidence in their tomb, however, we can surmise something of the world in which the brothers lived. They were clearly sons of privilege. By the late 12th Dynasty — as precise a guess as we can make for the tomb's date — the power of the nomarchs was waning as the pharaoh consolidated power and centralized political control. It seems unlikely that Khnum-Nakht's title of "great uab priest" involved much more than ceremonial duties at the local temple, since the term *uab* or *wab* translates as "pure one" and implies no particular importance. He may have occupied a sort of middle-management position, overseeing lesser priests. But the district governors remained personages of wealth and power, and the two brothers would have

former Egyptian courtier living in exile among the "Asiatics," who returns to Egypt in time to die and be buried according to Egyptian custom. By the late 12th Dynasty, the Middle Kingdom was at its height. Khnum-Nakht and his younger brother Nekht-Ankh lived in Egypt during one of its greatest ages.

On a contemporary visit to the Egyptian Gallery of the Manchester Museum, museum-goers can compare the Two Brothers' actual skulls with their reconstructed heads (above) and examine these beautifully preserved sculptures (opposite), among them likenesses of the brothers themselves.

lived in comfort and been treated with the deference accorded to local aristocrats.

Because they lived at some distance from the political and cultural centers, it is difficult to know to what degree the two brothers were exposed to the great artistic flowering of the 12th Dynasty (the Middle Kingdom), which Egyptologists generally regard as the classical age of Egyptian art and literature, the equivalent of Shakespeare's time in the history of English literature. From this period come many famous works, including the great epic novel *The Story of Sinuhe*, which tells the tale of a

But none of our knowledge of the 12th Dynasty helps explain the mystery of these two men. A burial of two brothers is not unknown but it is unusual. Whatever their blood relationship, other evidence in the tomb suggests a bond of deep affection. Within each of the coffins, Petrie found a small statue of the other brother. Perhaps DNA analysis will someday help us solve this puzzle. More likely, the true relationship of the two men found in the Tomb of the Two Brothers will remain a fascinating subject of conjecture.

—*Rosalie David*

CHAPTER TWO

OUT OF THE MUMMY'S TOMB

EGYPTIAN MUMMIES BEGAN APPEARING IN EUROPE AS SOUVENIRS AS EARLY AS THE 17TH CENTURY, but for the previous several hundred years, European doctors had prescribed a costly drug called *mumia* for many ills. *Mumia* was the Persian word for bitumen, a substance derived from mineral pitch that had been used by ancient doctors to treat medical problems ranging from gout to leprosy. When doctors seeking new sources of *mumia* to meet the demand encountered the preserved bodies of ancient Egyptians, they mistook the darkened resin that coated the wrappings for bitumen. Before long, this resinous carapace came to stand for the whole body, and *mumia*, or "mummy," became a coveted potion manufactured by grinding up the mummy — human remains, resin, wrapping, and all. So popular was *mumia* in the 16th century that King Francis I of France is said never to have left home without it. (He took it in a mixture with ground rhubarb.) And in 1714, the great English scientist Francis Bacon would write, "mummy hath great force in staunching blood." By the time mummy was discarded as medicine, the word had come to stand for the body itself, which is why we now refer to the preserved remains of the ancient Egyptians — and by extension all bodies preserved by natural or artificial means — as mummies.

Napoleon Bonaparte exhorts his troops before the Battle of the Pyramids, while the wonders of Egypt shimmer in the background. In truly heroic exaggeration, this dramatic 19th-century painting gives no hint of the miserable outcome of Napoleon's Egyptian adventure.

The leap from medieval superstition to the birth of mummy science seems a long one and would certainly have been delayed further had it not been for Napoleon Bonaparte's ill-conceived attempt to conquer Egypt in 1798. The future emperor had barely landed his troops when the British imposed a naval blockade that choked off supplies and severely hampered his communication with the Directorate back in Paris. Early military success gave way to a series of grinding defeats, exacerbated

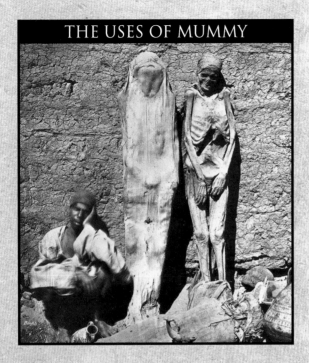

THE USES OF MUMMY

During the Middle Ages, medicine made from mummies was in such demand that Egyptian exporters often substituted recently executed criminals for ancient bodies. These were dried in the desert sun so as to resemble real mummies. As a drug, *mumia* was prescribed for a range of ailments, including abscesses, fractures, concussions, paralysis, epilepsy, coughs, nausea, and ulcers. Not every medieval physician was convinced, however, of its healing properties. The famous surgeon Ambroise Paré found the cure worse than the complaint: "This wicked kinde of drugge, doth nothing to help the diseased . . . it also inferres many troublesome symptomes, as the paine of the heart or stomacke, vomiting, and stinke of the mouth."

Long after apothecaries ceased grinding up mummies for medicine, people found other uses for them. In 19th-century Egypt they were still so abundant that peasants used them for firewood and artists ground them up to make a pigment called Mummy Brown. Mark Twain even claimed that in Egypt they were used as fuel for steam locomotives.

by the parasitical diseases that decimated troops unaccustomed to tropical ailments. A large proportion of his men contracted a parasitical eye disease that left them blind and which has been known ever since as ophthalmia militensis. Many were also afflicted with the waterborne bilharzia parasite, which remains epidemic in Egypt today.

The only two lasting results of Bonaparte's ego-driven misadventure were the political reawakening of Egypt — then a subject state of the Ottoman Empire — and the discovery of ancient Egypt by contemporary Europeans. The pyramids and the ruined temples along the Nile astonished the French troops. Before the Battle of the Pyramids in July 1798, Napoleon egged on his troops with this exhortation: "Soldiers, forty centuries are looking down upon you!" After Napoleon's troops returned to France, their tales of wonder would soon have faded had it not been for the cadre of 175 "learned civilians" the future emperor had brought along to adorn his expected triumph.

Among these proto-Egyptologists traveled an artist of modest talent but acute eye and impeccable draftsmanship, Dominique Vivant Denon. Baron Denon, as he had been known before the Revolution, was 51 when he arrived in Egypt, but he exhibited the energy of a dervish in his efforts to record what he saw. On one occasion, he put down his sketchbook only long enough to shoot a Mameluke sniper who was taking aim at his head. Denon's careful drawings became the principal attraction of his *Travels in Lower and Upper Egypt*, published in 1802 in French and soon translated into English and German. The book caused a sensation in Europe, helping give birth to two inextricably linked phenomena: Egyptian tourism and Egyptology. (The ensuing years saw the publication of a massive scholarly series, *Description de l'Égypte*, which exhaustively chronicled the work of the scholars Napoleon took with him to Egypt.)

Two hundred years after the publication of Denon's *Travels*, it is difficult to comprehend the depth of Europe's ignorance about ancient Egypt at the dawn of the Industrial Revolution. Almost 1,500 years had passed since the last Egyptian lived who could read or write hieroglyphs. The secret of the ancient Egyptian language seemed irretrievably lost — and with it the key to a civilization that had flourished for roughly three thousand years. But near Rosetta in the Nile Delta, French troops had unearthed a tablet of black basalt bearing inscriptions in three scripts: ancient Greek, Demotic (a simplified version of Hieratic, itself a cursive form of hieroglyphs), and hieroglyphs. The soldiers sent the Rosetta Stone to the scholars settled in Cairo, who immediately recognized it as the key to solving the language puzzle.

Dominique Vivant Denon, seen here in a self-portrait with strangely out-of-proportion pyramids in the background, contributed to the remarkable record Napoleon brought home from Egypt. On his return, he helped advise the future emperor about which works of art to pillage from the countries he conquered, a collection that today graces the Louvre.

Breaking the ancient code was no simple matter, however, requiring nearly 30 years of international intellectual competition. In the end, victory went to a remarkable Frenchman by the name of Jean-François Champollion, a self-taught linguist. As with so many brainteasers that look easy once solved, the obstacle lay in an obvious but false assumption: Since hieroglyphs were clearly based on pictographs, the script must be ideographic, not phonetic. Champollion's breakthrough came only after he hypothesized that these ancient characters were in fact a combination of phonetically spelled words and pictographs, but primarily a complex phonetic alphabet. It would be many more years before scholars would become reasonably fluent in ancient Egyptian, but breaking the Rosetta code made Egyptology possible.

IN THE FIRST HALF OF THE 19TH CENTURY, AS MORE AND MORE EUROPEAN TOURISTS CAME AND WENT, what one historian has aptly called "the rape of Egypt" grew into a kind of archeological gold rush. Priceless remnants of Egypt's pharaonic age could simply be plucked out of the sand.

THE RAPE OF EGYPT

No 19th-century tour of Egypt was complete without some ancient souvenirs secreted in one's baggage for the return trip. European tourists ransacked tombs, sometimes tearing off a mummy's limb if the whole body seemed too much to carry. One of the more amusing stories of mummy smuggling comes from the diary of a very proper Victorian Englishwoman named Miss Marianne Brocklehurst, who traveled with her companion, Miss Booth, to Egypt. In the course of their travels they made arrangements to acquire a mummy from an Arab dealer. Here is their description of the mummy's nocturnal delivery: "Presently, we saw them coming down the bank carrying the horrid thing wrapped in a black cloth, all in the bright moonshine. . . . The Mummy was deposited in the passage where one of us stumbled over it in the dark, the bearer was thrust out of the window and all was over!"

Many more professional visitors amassed considerable fortunes by pillaging the tombs of the dead, then selling the artifacts to collectors and museums. The art museums of many a European capital now boast fine Egyptian collections founded on such plunder.

(Above) Turn-of-the-century tourists strike an obligatory pose before the pyramids. (Left and right) Essential to any visit was an attempt to scale the great monuments, most often accomplished with the assistance of hired porters, who hauled panting visitors up the crumbling façades.

The produce of plundered tombs made a handsome living for many an Egyptian entrepreneur, and it seemed that no early-19th-century visitor left Egypt without a trunkful of ancient objects. Some left with boatloads. Many left with mummies.

It was professional plunder, however, that did the most damage. Even the early excavators were little better than tomb robbers, and most collectors cared nothing for the context, mesmerized as they were by the value or exoticism of the objects gathered. The most spectacularly successful

Swashbuckler and showman Giovanni Belzoni (left) brought Egypt to the masses. Along with mummies, statues, and other more portable treasures, he oversaw the removal of colossal works of art from Egypt, including the head of the "young Memnon," (Ramesses II) from the Ramesseum at Thebes (right).

of these early treasure hunters were a naturalized Frenchman of Italian origin named Bernardino Drovetti and the English landscape painter Henry Salt, who served for many years as British consul in Egypt. Salt and Drovetti, who styled themselves dealers in antiquities, collectively acquired the thousands of artifacts that founded the splendid Egyptian collections in the great museums of Paris, London, Turin, and Berlin. Both became rich men as a result.

Some of these 19th-century profit seekers took a more than passing interest in the ancient civilization being pillaged, the most famous being Giovanni Battista Belzoni, a former music-hall strongman. Belzoni began collecting as an agent for Henry Salt, then struck out on his own, building a reputation for retrieving and transporting colossal statuary, including the giant bust of Ramesses II that now graces the Egyptian Sculpture Hall of the British Museum. Although a complete archeological amateur, he kept a lively record of his exploits, which he published in his memoir *Narrative of the Operations and Recent Discoveries within the Pyramids, Temples, Tombs and Excavations in Egypt and Nubia*, illustrated with his own evocative watercolors. In the fall of 1817, Belzoni made the first great discovery in the Valley of the Kings west of Thebes, the tomb of Sethos I (1318-1304 B.C.E.), father of Ramesses the Great.

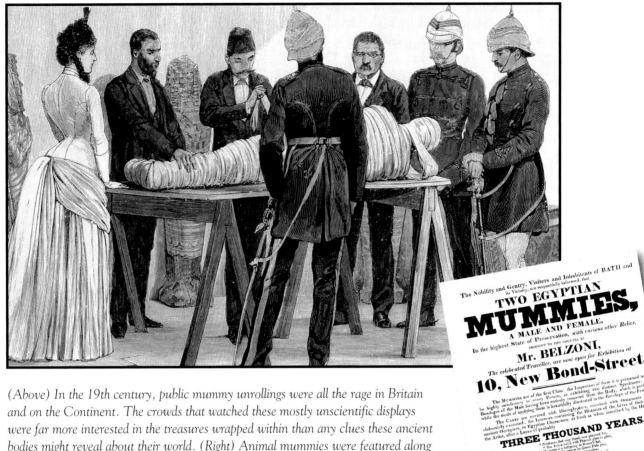

(Above) In the 19th century, public mummy unrollings were all the rage in Britain and on the Continent. The crowds that watched these mostly unscientific displays were far more interested in the treasures wrapped within than any clues these ancient bodies might reveal about their world. (Right) Animal mummies were featured along with those of humans in this Belzoni double bill.

The tomb of Sethos had been empty for three millennia and the pharaoh's mummy had disappeared, but Belzoni the showman knew a golden opportunity when it chanced along. In London in the spring of 1821, inside the recently erected Egyptian Hall in Piccadilly, he built a replica of the pharaoh's last resting place as a backdrop for the exhibit's *pièce de résistance*, the sarcophagus of the pharaoh Sethos I. The show benefited from the publication of his book the previous year, but Belzoni wasn't taking any chances.

Before he opened the tomb of Sethos to the general public, he staged a clever invitation-only promotion event. With an audience of eminent doctors looking on, he unwrapped the mummy of a young man. Belzoni was by no means the first European to "unroll" a mummy, but he seems to have been one of the first to turn an Egyptian mummy into a prop for public entertainment.

The Italian-born entrepreneur wouldn't rate even a footnote in the annals of paleopathology, however, had it not been for his impact on one of the physicians present at the London unrolling, Thomas Pettigrew. A highly respected member of London's medical establishment, Pettigrew couldn't get Belzoni's mummy out of his mind, so he attended two more unwrappings staged by the master showman. In 1833, when Henry Salt's personal collection of Egyptian booty went on auction, Pettigrew and a friend each purchased a mummy. On April 6, Pettigrew unrolled both of them in a packed lecture hall at Charing Cross Hospital, where he held the Chair of Anatomy.

The response was rapturous and the doctor was hooked. Over the next year, Mummy Pettigrew, as he came to be called, staged a series of unwrappings — for a while these became known as the "mummy of the month" — before standing-room-only audiences. His public success launched such a mummy craze that in mid-Victorian England, a country weekend for members of the English gentry might very well include among its enticements a mummy unwrapping. This English mania was part of a broader Europe-wide phenomenon, and in 1833, a French visitor to the court of the Egyptian viceroy Mohammed Ali commented, "It would hardly be respectable, on one's return from Egypt, to present oneself in Europe without a mummy in one hand and a crocodile in the other."

Pettigrew may have helped fuel the craze, and contemporary accounts demonstrate that he knew how to play a crowd, but he was much more than a faddist or a showman. He kept careful notes of every unwrapping and treated each autopsy as a scientific, as well as a theatrical, exercise. In 1834, he published the first serious study of mummies and methods of mummification, *A History of Egyptian Mummies*, with illustrations by George Cruikshank, who later became Dickens' illustrator.

G. Elliot Smith, who examined many mummies in the first decade of the 20th century, described the book as "a monument of exact observation," and many years later, Aidan Cockburn, a modern British pioneer of mummy science working in the United States, was so impressed with Pettigrew's work that he would write the following: "In 1834, technology was in its infancy, so that, for example, parasites and disease-forming bacteria were almost unknown. Yet within his limitations, Pettigrew has followed almost identically the path taken by our own group in studying mummies. The descriptions, the insects, the question of cotton, attempts at biochemistry with no less a scientist than Michael Farraday, the discussion of mummies outside Egypt — all these were included, so that his work is almost a blueprint for ours. . . . It is humbling to realize that apart from the use of such modern tools as the electron microscope, X-rays, and chromatographs, almost all today's work was anticipated by Pettigrew a century and a half ago."

THOMAS PETTIGREW MAY BE THE PROTOTYPE OF THE CONTEMPORARY PALEOPATHOLOGIST, BUT he was by no means the first to apply scientific methods to ancient tissue. As early as 1718, the German apothecary Christian Herzog unwrapped a mummy and published his findings. (After the autopsy, he probably ground up the mummy to make medicine.) In the 1790s, a German doctor and anthropologist named Johann Blumenbach unwrapped half the mummies in the British Museum. In the early 1820s, an English physician named Augustus Granville performed a mummy autopsy at his country house over the course of several weeks, keeping careful notes and concluding that the cause of death was uterine cancer. (It is now believed the tumor was benign.) Britain's earliest multidisciplinary unwrapping took place in Leeds in 1825, where a team of specialists, including physicians, anatomists, and a chemist, examined the late-20th-Dynasty (1200-1085 B.C.E.) mummy of a priest called Natsef-Amun. But none of these or other early investigators were able to look beyond the surface of dried flesh and fragile bone. The next stage of mummy science would have to wait for scientists such as Louis Pasteur to gain an understanding of the true nature of disease, the real beginning of modern medicine. These scientific advances were accompanied by improvements in medical technology, including better microscopes and the invention of the X-ray.

After Giovanni Battista Belzoni, the pirates of the early 19th century continued their plunder of Egyptian treasure until the advent of the French archeologist Auguste Mariette. No mean excavator himself, Mariette's real legacy comes from his efforts at conservation. Before Mariette, there was little or no attempt at *in situ* conservation, which meant objects untouched by oxygen for thousands of years often disintegrated soon after they reached daylight. Mariette tried to put a stop to this by pioneering the use of conservation workshops at excavation sites so that recovered objects could be treated before being transported. In 1858, he was appointed director of the fledgling Egyptian Antiquities Service and the same year founded the Bulaq Museum (now the Egyptian Museum, Cairo). Thenceforth, no piece of ancient Egypt could legally leave the country without first being offered to him or his successors. Much illegal booty continued to evade the authorities, but the totally unchecked trade in ancient artifacts ceased.

Nevertheless, neither Mariette nor any of his mid-19th-century contemporaries practiced a brand of archeology that would pass muster today. When they dug, they dug for the glamorous,

AUGUSTE MARIETTE

Many years after Auguste Mariette had settled in Egypt, he would remark, "The Egyptian duck is a dangerous animal: one snap of its beak and you are infected with Egyptology for life." The duck to which Mariette referred was a hieroglyphic drawing of a duck that had captured his imagination in the 1840s when he was still a teacher at the Collège de Boulogne. Soon after he finally arrived in Egypt in 1850, he made an astonishing discovery: the Serapeum at Memphis. Other great discoveries followed. But his greatest legacy is as the founder of the Egyptian Antiquities Service and of the collection that was the forerunner to the present-day Cairo Museum.

the beautiful, the valuable, the translatable. Each tended to be obsessed with a narrow aspect of the ancient world, ignoring all the rest. None made a careful plan of the excavation site before beginning to dig. None kept a careful record of where and in what context each item was found.

This undisciplined state of affairs appalled the young Flinders Petrie when he first arrived in Egypt in 1880. As an almost complete autodidact, Petrie saw Egypt through eyes mostly unburdened by conventional wisdom, and he carried in his kit a combination of skills foreign to most Egyptologists of his day. He was a fine mathematician who helped invent the practice of statistics, a more than competent surveyor, a skilled photographer, and a man of great ingenuity and encyclopedic memory. If he never mastered Greek or Latin and never learned to read hieroglyphs fluently, he virtually invented systematic archeological excavation.

On a dig, Petrie overlooked nothing, however inconsequential it might have seemed to others. Almost from the start, he took a special interest in pottery, which led him to what many regard as his most important contribution to the history of his profession, which he called Sequence Dating. He accomplished this by means of a careful analysis of the styles of pots he had meticulously gathered from nine hundred pre-dynastic tombs at three different sites. His system was soon applied by other archeologists and is today known as Seriation. Thanks to Petrie, archeologists learned to date a site by the style of pottery found at each level of the excavation. With modifications, Petrie's method is still in use today.

While Petrie's discoveries included much that was grand and romantic, including the pyramid of the Middle Kingdom (1991-1786 B.C.E.) pharaoh Amenemhet III and an incomparable trove of New Kingdom art at el 'Amarna, he also dug in places where ordinary people lived — notably, the town of Kahun, which housed the workers who had built the Middle Kingdom tomb of Senusret II, the Pyramid of Lahun. It was the first such town discovered and is still one of the few known ancient sites that was neither tomb nor temple. By excavating this settlement, he collected a wealth of objects from everyday life.

Unlike most of his contemporaries, Petrie showed an interest in the mummies he found, as well as the objects that were buried with them. Here is his description of an Old Kingdom (ca. 2686-2181 B.C.E.) mummy found near Medum in 1891: "The mode of embalming was very singular. The body was shrunk, wrapped in a linen cloth, then modeled all over with resin, into the natural form and plumpness of the living figure, completely restoring all the fullness of the form, and this was wrapped around in a few turns of finest gauze. The eyes and eyebrows were painted on the outer wrapping with green."

The indefatigable Petrie was also among the first to take something like an X-ray of a mummified body. (A German scientist named König was actually the first: he photographed a mummy with a roentgen machine — an early form of X-ray — in 1896.) In 1897, Petrie brought back to University College, where he was on the faculty, the disarticulated bones — each of them wrapped separately before being placed in the coffin — of a mummy from an Old Kingdom burial site. In London they were examined by the university's Anatomy Department and photographed with a roentgen machine. According to Petrie, the results supported his sensational and subsequently discredited theory that the bones showed signs of cannibalism, possibly of a ritual nature. The following year, he X-rayed a whole mummy in Cairo.

BY THE BEGINNING OF THE 20TH CENTURY, A NEW GENERATION OF EGYPTOLOGISTS HAD ADOPTED and refined Petrie's methods and applied them with even greater rigor. The newly respectable science of Egyptology provided the context for the discoveries of the three founding fathers of 20th-century paleopathology, Grafton Elliot Smith, Alfred Lucas, and Sir Marc Armand Ruffer. The three arrived on the scene around 1900, when they took up professorships at the Government School of Medicine in Cairo, a product of the stable British protectorate under which Egypt was then governed. The three colleagues each stood at the acme of his profession. Smith was a renowned anatomist and anthropologist, Lucas a distinguished chemist, and Ruffer a specialist in bacteriology, with a particular interest in histopathology, the analysis of tissue for evidence of disease. Innately curious individuals, the three were fascinated by the ancient world, whose remains lay everywhere around them. As scientists, they were inevitably

Sir Flinders Petrie (opposite) did much to modernize archeology. His system for dating a site by the period of its pottery inaugurated the first accurate archeological dating system. Petrie's successors included the three founders of modern paleopathology: Grafton Elliot Smith (right); Alfred Lucas (middle); and Marc Armand Ruffer. Ruffer, the son of a French baron, who had trained at Oxford, died in 1916 when his ship was lost at sea. Elliot Smith went on to hold the Chair of Anthropology at Manchester University. Lucas stayed in Egypt and continued his research.

drawn to the primary source of scientific specimens, mummies.

By the turn of the century, the Egyptian Museum, founded 40 years earlier by Auguste Mariette, housed the remains of many royal, noble, and priestly figures. But circumstances were about to conspire to create a mummy inundation. In 1902, the first Aswan Dam would be completed, flooding large areas of the Upper Nile Valley. As a result, hundreds of sites and thousands of mummies would vanish beneath the rising waters. Elliot Smith led a team of medical specialists who examined and autopsied thousands of mummies before the dam was completed, in the process of which "the pathologies of ancient Egypt were laid bare," in the words of paleopathologist Aidan Cockburn.

The first royal mummy Smith examined came from the tomb of the 18th-Dynasty (1567-1320 B.C.E.) pharaoh Amenhotep II, discovered early in 1898 in the Valley of the Kings near Thebes, the ancient capital, situated in Upper Egypt. It was the mummy of the pharaoh's son and successor, Tuthmosis IV. (Originally, each New Kingdom (18th to 20th Dynasties) royal mummy had been interred in a separate royal tomb carved out of the rock, but many were later moved to secret group tombs for safety after their individual resting places were discovered and disturbed by thieves.) At the invitation of Gaston Maspero, Mariette's successor as head of the museum and director of the Antiquities Service, Smith performed the autopsy at the ceremonial unwrapping of this mummy, which took place on March 26, 1903.

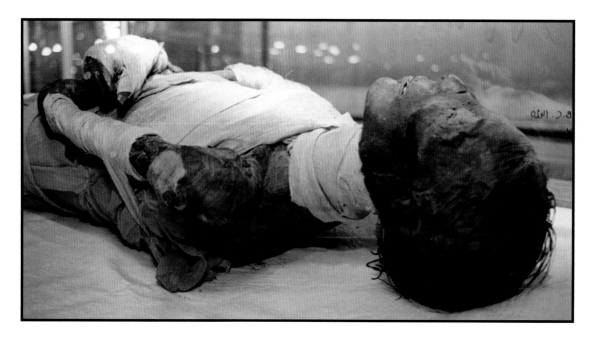

In his own time Tuthmosis IV was celebrated as the architect of a peace accord between Egypt and its chief rival, the Mitannian Empire. Today, his unwrapped remains (above) rest in the Cairo Museum, bearing scant resemblance to the monumental black granite bust of the pharaoh (opposite).

Present at the event were an invited audience of the local elite and a young Englishman named Howard Carter, already making a name for himself as an archeologist to watch. But according to Smith's biographer, the doctor "found it impossible, under such spectacular circumstances, to make more than a very superficial examination of the body, and in order to furnish 'une évaluation exacte,' he requested Maspero to allow him to make a detailed examination in private." Maspero agreed.

Of particular interest to Maspero and other Egyptologists was the age at which Tuthmosis IV had died, information that would help confirm the chronology of his reign. In order to make an

accurate estimate, Smith needed to perform an X-ray, but the only X-ray machine in Cairo belonged to a nursing home. In later years, the story of the X-ray of Tuthmosis IV became one of Elliot Smith's best after-dinner anecdotes. It went something like this:

Before the day in question, Smith enlisted Howard Carter to help him transport Tuthmosis IV to the nursing home. The two carefully carried the rigid mummy from the museum to a waiting horse-drawn cab, then laid the pharaoh across their laps for the ride through Cairo's crowded streets. At the nursing home, the mummy was X-rayed by a Dr. Khayat, then returned by cab to the museum.

So pleased was Gaston Maspero with Smith's work on Tuthmosis IV that he gave him virtually unlimited access to the mummies in the museum, royal or otherwise. The results were catalogued in Elliot Smith's *Royal Mummies* (1912), which helped pave the way to his classic work on the history of mummification, *Egyptian Mummies* (1924), a book he co-wrote with W.R. Dawson, a colleague during the Aswan rescue project.

The second founding father, chemist Alfred Lucas, was as interested in the process of mummification as he was in its evolution. It was he who first debunked the standard translation of Herodotus's famous account of mummification, dating from the 2nd century B.C.E. The Greek historian, often relying on second- and third-hand sources, described the cadaver being immersed in a liquid bath of natron. Lucas's book *Ancient Egyptian Materials and Industries* (first published in 1926) devotes a major chapter to mummification. In it he concludes forcefully, "the phraseology of Herodotus, Diodorus, and Athenaeus and other [ancient] writers makes it perfectly clear that the ancient Egyptian process of embalming the human body was analogous to that for preserving fish." In other words, the ancient embalmers used natron in its solid, not its liquid, form. Lucas spent many years gathering mummy evidence to support his claim, even performing experimental mummification of small animals. Only solid natron produced the desired result.

Of the three pioneers, however, Marc Armand Ruffer, one of the first to look at mummy tissue under a microscope, did the most to lay the foundation for modern disease studies. Born in France and educated in England, Ruffer faced a tricky problem: Unlike living or recently deceased human tissue, mummy tissue is extremely difficult to work with. In consistency it is either tough and leathery or extremely friable. Before it can be examined microscopically, it has to be restored to a more malleable state.

Ruffer experimented with various chemical combinations for rehydrating ancient tissue, finally coming up with a simple solution of alcohol, water, and carbonate of soda that consistently worked well. The rehydrated tissue could then be sliced thin enough for microscopic examination, and under a microscope it resembled living tissue to a remarkable degree. As a result of his microscopic studies, Ruffer was, for example, the first to discover unmistakable evidence of ancient bilharziasis, or schistosomiasis, in the form of parasite eggs in tissue samples from the kidneys of two 20th-Dynasty (1200-1085 B.C.E.) mummies. So successful was Ruffer at studying tissue from ancient Egyptian mummies that his rehydrating solution became known as Ruffer's Solution. A variation of it is used today by many paleohistologists.

Lucas lived in Egypt until his death in 1945, but Smith and Ruffer soon departed, Ruffer dying tragically in a war-related shipwreck in the Mediterranean in 1916. Their work endured, however, so that when Howard Carter made his renowned discovery of the Tomb of King Tutankhamen in 1922, it was taken for granted that the pharaoh's mummy would receive a rigorous scientific examination. Less than a year after Carter and his patron Lord Carnarvon had first entered the tomb's antechamber, Elliot Smith wrote that "the chief interest of the discovery should be in the mummy itself, for the welfare of which all the elaborate arrangements were made. It is not merely because mummies enable us to form some idea of the physical features of the kings and queens, and by appealing to our common humanity give their personalities a reality they would not otherwise possess; nor is it because they often reveal evidence of age and infirmities; their chief interest is the light they throw on the history of the period and upon the development of the art of embalming."

Howard Carter's insistence on methodically photographing, recording, and conserving all the objects found in King Tut's tomb, before removing them, set a new — and much higher — standard for archeological practice.

Not until November 1925, three years after Howard Carter unearthed the entrance to Tutankhamen's tomb, would the pharaoh's mummified remains be revealed. First the tomb's antechambers had to be exhaustively catalogued and their contents removed, then the burial chamber entered and its contents likewise listed, labeled, and carted carefully away. Only then was Carter ready to tackle the king's massive sarcophagus, carved from a single block of yellow quartzite with a lid made of rose-colored granite. Within the sarcophagus lay three coffins, nested one inside the other, each one more magnificent than its predecessor. The final coffin was wrought of solid gold. Finally, the lid was gently lifted away.

The first of Tutankhamen's three coffins (left) was made of gilded wood. His solid gold innermost coffin was covered with an almost impenetrable layer of hardened unguents. To break the seal (above), Howard Carter employed hammers, solvents, and heat. (Below right) Inside the third coffin was the mummy of the pharaoh, adorned with a magnificent gold portrait mask. (Below left) As Carter, seen second from left, bends forward to get a better look, Douglas Derry makes the first incision through the boy king's wrappings.

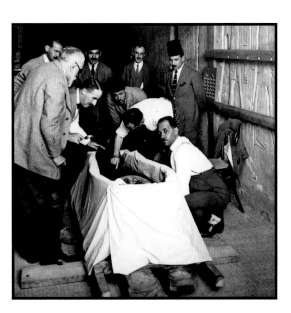

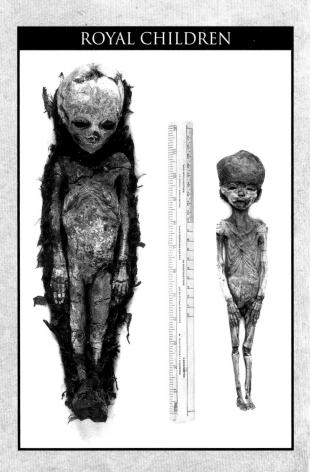

ROYAL CHILDREN

In a simple wooden box in small room off King Tut's burial chamber, Howard Carter discovered two tiny wooden coffins, each containing the remains of a still-born baby girl: one of five months' and one of about seven months' gestation. Douglas Derry examined the bodies — observing that an attempt had clearly been made to embalm the older child — but left no report of what he found. A more recent autopsy has revealed that the older child may have suffered from a congenital condition known as Sprengel's deformity, characterized by a small, high shoulder blade, spina bifida, and scoliosis. Though their tiny anthropoid coffins offer no clue to their identities, the two girls are almost certainly the premature daughters of the boy king and his young wife, Ankhesenamun.

"At such moments the emotions evade verbal expression," Carter later wrote. "Three thousand years and more had elapsed since men's eyes had gazed into that golden coffin. Time, measured by the brevity of human life, seemed to lose its common perspectives before a spectacle so vividly recalling the solemn religious rites of a vanished civilization. . . . Here at last lay all that was left of the youthful Pharaoh, hitherto little more to us than the shadow of a name."

Until this juncture, the King Tut story had unfolded according to some ideal script. Now it took an undesirable turn. As each of the precious objects inside the coffin was removed, "the more evident it became that the covering wrappings and the mummy were both in a parlous state. They were completely carbonized by the action that had been set up by the fatty acids of the unguents with which they had been saturated." Thus the story of the single richest find in the history of Egyptian archeology ended in anticlimax. In contrast to the many royal mummies previously recovered — Tutankhamen had been anointed so lavishly that a combustion reaction had occurred inside the coffin. Even though the mummy was undisturbed, the wrappings and the body inside had burned up leaving little more than bones and ashes.

So friable was the mummy that it could not be moved. It fell to Douglas Derry of the Egyptian University, a former student of Smith, to conduct the anatomical examination on the spot. Derry made the most of his opportunity.

Many have seen some likeness between the pharaoh Akhenaten (above) and his supposed son Tutankhamen (below). So far the mummy of Akhenaten has never been found. Until it is, their kinship cannot be conclusively proven.

"The examination of the young king afforded no clue to the cause of his early death," he reported, but it did provide two fascinating pieces of evidence about his life.

Derry was familiar with the mummy found in Tomb 55 in the Valley of the Kings, discovered in 1907 by a wealthy American. At the time, many people believed the mummy belonged to Akhenaten, but by the time King Tut was discovered it was thought to belong to Akhenaten's brother Smenkhkare. Akhenaten was the famous heretic pharaoh who briefly and unsuccessfully attempted to impose on his subjects the worship of a single god, Aten, the disc of the sun. He also may have been Tutankhamen's father or his half-brother. From the marked similarities between Tut's skull and the skull of the mummy in Tomb 55 — both had unusually broad and flat-topped heads — Derry was able to conclude that they were closely related. He also decided, after examining the degree of bone development, that the pharaoh had died between the ages of 17 and 19, most likely at the age of 18 years.

MUMMY SCIENCE MADE LITTLE PROGRESS FROM THE 1930s TO THE EARLY 1970s. In part, this hiatus may have stemmed from the advent of the Great Depression, World War II, and the Arab-Israeli conflict, but it also probably reflects a preoccupation among Egyptologists with language and archeology. There were notable exceptions: In the 1960s a team spearheaded by dental scientists from the University of Michigan carried out the first major X-ray studies of mummies outside Egypt. During the same decade, Scottish paleopathologist Andrew T. Sandison, a pathologist at Glasgow's Royal Infirmary, refined Ruffer's methods for softening mummy tissue, allowing it to be sectioned for microscopic examination.

Not until the early 1970s would the study of ancient diseases through the examination of ancient bodies become a major interdisciplinary activity involving hundreds of researchers around the world. The Manchester Mummy Research Project quickly established itself as one of the leaders in this field, but it was part of this much larger phenomenon.

A CONVERSATION WITH SIR FLINDERS PETRIE

When I was an undergraduate at University College London, the ghost of Sir William Matthews Flinders Petrie haunted the air we breathed. Even during his life, Petrie was a legend, and by the early 1960s, his legend had grown large. One of my tutors, Margaret Drower, would go on to write the only biography of Petrie, *A Life in*

Archaeology. It is as thorough and down-to-earth a record of an amazingly full career as one could hope for, but it does not neglect the romantic side. Undoubtedly he served as one of the models for the dashing screen archeologist Indiana Jones.

One of my favorite stories about Petrie dates from his very first trip to Egypt in 1880, when he was all of 27. He wasted no time in getting down to work, which in this case was to take measurements inside the Great Pyramid in order to test a theory then enjoying a certain celebrity. According to the famous British astronomer Piazzi Smyth, the Great Pyramid was a work of divine inspiration that contained within its corridors and chambers a sort of map of the past and the future and held many of the secrets of science.

Petrie seems to have thought nothing of setting up living quarters in an abandoned mastaba — the tomb of an Egyptian noble — and seems to

(Previous page) A rather romanticized view of Petrie marshaling his Egyptian fieldworkers into archeological battle. (Right) An elderly Petrie with some of the pottery he used in developing his Sequence Dating technique. He is also credited with the discovery of the world's oldest linen garment (opposite), a linen shirt or dress with a carefully pleated yoke from roughly 2980 B.C.E.

have adapted effortlessly to the primitive amenities it afforded: "Life here is really comfortable," he wrote a friend, "without many of the encumbrances of regular hours: bells, collars and cuffs, blacking, tablecloths or many other of the unnecessaries of Civilisation."

Like most European visitors to Egypt, Petrie had wisely arrived during winter. But as anyone who has entered the Great Pyramid will know, it is a stuffy airless place at the best of times, and the young Flinders found it almost unbearable. To mitigate the problem, he made all his interior

measurements at night when the air was coolest. And according to legend, since there was no one around to see him or to stop him, he simply removed all his clothes and entered the pharaoh's tomb stark naked. Each night Petrie spent long hours with tape measure, pencil, and notebook, emerging just before dawn, red-eyed, oxygen-deprived, and smelling of bat dung.

For Petrie, the facts always came first, and unfortunately for Smyth's theory, Petrie's measurements didn't add up — a conclusion he published broadly in his first book, *The Pyramids and Temples of Giza* (1883). His 90 books and hundreds of published articles and reviews are filled with facts — no Egyptologist has equaled his record of prompt publication — and remarkably devoid of self-congratulation, despite his long list of accomplishments. While still a relatively young man, he was granted a professorship at University College, even though he had never attended a high school, let alone a university.

His memoir, *Seventy Years in Egyptology*, is often a rather dry chronicle of expeditions and artifacts, but occasionally the real Petrie peeps through, as in this passage quoted from his diary, which describes his sleeping quarters during excavations of a temple site at Medinet el Fayumn in 1888: "I daresay many folks think it is a very pleasant and easy sort of life in a tent; and so it would be if room were unlimited. Imagine being limited to a space six and a half feet long, and about as wide as the length, and you have the ground plan of my square tent, sloping up to nothing, at less than standing height. Besides [a] bed I have nine boxes in it, stores of all kinds, basin, cooking stove and crockery, tripod stand (serving for clothes) and bag and portmanteau, and some antiques; and in this I have to live, to sleep, to wash, and to receive visitors. I tried to get a rather larger tent, but in all the bazaar there was none, unless I had one of ninety pounds weight, instead of thirty, and that was too cumbrous." To this delightful description he appends the comment, "Important mummies were put under my bed."

Among his students at University College was Margaret Murray, one of the first women to practice Egyptology and a staunch feminist in her day. In her autobiography, *My First Hundred Years*, she leaves us a vivid portrait of Petrie, just back from his latest excavation in Egypt. He did not impress her on first encounter: "A big, black-bearded man was striding about, laughing and talking with a couple of strangers and behaving for all the world as if the whole place belonged to him."

Murray later changed her tune. Petrie became her mentor. "As soon as I got to know Petrie I realized that his was a type of mind entirely different from any I had encountered before. It is a fact that working with a genius alters all one's sense of values, for genius is not the same thing as talent. There are degrees of talent, but there are no degrees in genius, either it is there complete, or it is not there . . ."

I've always regretted that I never met Margaret Murray. She lived to be over a hundred and was still a presence at University College almost until the day she died in 1963, so I missed meeting her by only a few years. To my frustration, she doesn't even mention her time in Manchester, or her pioneering autopsy of the Two Brothers, in her autobiography. I would like to have asked her about these things. And I would like to have asked her about Flinders Petrie. What a remarkable man he must have been.

—*Rosalie David*

63

THE MAKING OF MUMMIES

THE ANCIENT EGYPTIAN ART OF EMBALMING — MUMMIFICATION — HAS ITS ROOTS IN THE PRE-HISTORY OF THE Nile Valley, when neolithic people buried their dead in shallow desert graves, where the combination of hot dry sand and lack of oxygen naturally desiccated the bodies. A number of these pre-dynastic "mummies" have been found, and some are remarkably well preserved. At some stage, the ancient Egyptians began to believe that bodily preservation was connected with immortality, and modern scholars assume that when the elite of the early dynasties began to be buried in tombs, they sought ways to preserve their bodies as perfectly as those that lay in the desert sand.

The idea of preserving the body for its voyage to the afterlife perfectly fits the precepts of ancient Egyptian religion as they have come down to us, including the fundamental story informing these funerary beliefs — the myth of Osiris. In mythological terms, Osiris was the first human being to be embalmed and reborn. But we do not know which came first, the myth or the mummy. Perhaps it doesn't really matter.

(Opposite) The elaborately decorated coffin of a man named Penju dates from around 800 B.C.E. From the coffin's inscriptions, we know that its occupant was a priest of the fertility god Min and that he lived in Middle Egypt. By the time this coffin was produced, the art of burial had progressed enormously from the days when pre-dynastic Egyptians interred their dead in shallow, desert graves. Of the pre-dynastic mummies that survive, one of the best preserved examples is "Ginger" (right), so named for his auburn hair. Ginger was wrapped in a reed mat and committed to the sands, along with his assortment of grave goods, around 3200 B.C.E.

A painting of Osiris, from the tomb of Sennejem, shows the god of death, resurrection, and fertility in his classic pose, holding the royal insignia of crook and flail. According to Egyptian belief, the more closely an embalmed body resembled Osiris, the first mummy, the better the person's chance of eternal life. By the time of Sennejem's death, probably during the reign of Ramesses II, the cult of Osiris was so developed that the figure of Osiris had become closely identified with the deceased — so much so, that the deceased was referred to as "The Osiris (name of deceased)" in much the same way that we might refer to "the late. . .".

The myth tells of a human king, Osiris — based, perhaps, on a real king from the First Dynasty (ca. 3100-2890 B.C.E.) — who brought agriculture and civilization to his people. Osiris was murdered by his jealous brother, Seth, who dismembered his body and scattered it far and wide. But Osiris's sister-wife, Isis, gathered his body back together, and with the help of Anubis, the jackal-headed god of embalming, restored him to life long enough to father their son Horus. When Horus grew to manhood, he challenged his uncle Seth so as to avenge his father's murder. Their dispute was settled before a tribunal of the gods, who decided in Osiris's favor and grant-

(Right) A vignette from the Book of the Dead depicts two of the essential aspects of a person that must make the journey into the afterlife with him: the winged figure represents the ba, or unique essence of the individual; the dark figure on the right is the person's shadow, who will protect the deceased from harm. (Above) A ba amulet dating from the 18th Dynasty (1567-1320 B.C.E.).

ed him eternal life, albeit as ruler of the underworld. Thus, the journey of Osiris from death to eternal life came to symbolize the journey from death to everlasting life in the next world, and his restored body became the archetype of the mummy.

The ancient Egyptians had two words for the essential human elements that must make the passage to the next world: the ba and the ka. The ba is sometimes mistakenly translated as "soul," but its meaning seems to be closer to "personality" or "character." The ka, on the other hand, is the life force. For a person to make the voyage into the next world, his ba and his ka must be able to reunite in his body. For this to happen, the physical body of the deceased must be preserved in as recognizable a form as possible.

Thus, mummification, the artificial preservation of a body after death, becomes a way of improving a person's chances of passage to the next world. (Since only a fraction of the population could afford mummification, even in later periods when it was widespread, Egyptian belief did not preclude the rebirth of anyone who had died with a virtuous heart.) From the beginning, the ancient embalmers strove toward two goals: to preserve the body as perfectly as possible and to render it as lifelike as possible.

While generally moving toward these ideals, the evolution of mummification roughly parallels the great

(Above) A depiction of the heart of the deceased being weighed against the feather of Maat, the goddess of truth. The ancient Egyptians believed that only those who had been honest in this life could make the journey into the land of eternal life. Note the jackal-headed god Anubis, who is adjusting the right-hand balance of the scale in the deceased's favor. (Opposite) A silver likeness of Psusennes I, the second ruler of the 21st Dynasty.

epochs of ancient Egyptian history. During periods of wealth and stability, embalming techniques tended to become more sophisticated. During periods of social turmoil and political instability, the practice of embalming tended to stand still or veer off in unexpected directions — sometimes leading to experimentation that would embellish standard practice during the next period of more orderly society.

Mummification is one of the most stable elements of Egyptian culture. In good times and bad, it was

practiced with dedication and great skill. Until the art reached its generally accepted peak in the 21st Dynasty (part of the Third Intermediate Period), between about 1089 and 525 B.C.E., it generally evolved toward these twin ideals. Not surprisingly, however, the early experiments in mummification yielded mixed results.

The embalmers of the Old Kingdom (3rd to 6th Dynasties, ca. 2686-ca. 2181 B.C.E.) concentrated on rendering the mummy wrappings as lifelike as possible, presumably since they hadn't yet learned how to preserve the flesh. The few surviving mummies from this era seldom reveal any serious attempts at preserving the body. At least as early as the 4th Dynasty, however, Old Kingdom embalmers began experimenting with natron, a naturally occurring compound of salts that is close in chemical composition to bicarbonate of soda. When a body was packed in natron crystals, the salt would draw out moisture from the tissue — in essentially the same way as it does when used for drying salt fish. But the consistent use of natron as a means of drying and preserving the body did not occur until the Middle Kingdom (12th Dynasty, 1991-1786 B.C.E.).

To generalize from scanty evidence, Old Kingdom mummies — all of them belonging to royalty or nobility — share a handful of salient

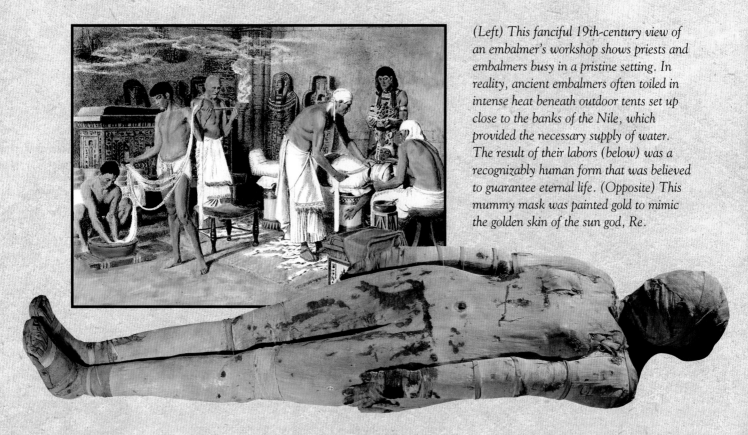

(Left) This fanciful 19th-century view of an embalmer's workshop shows priests and embalmers busy in a pristine setting. In reality, ancient embalmers often toiled in intense heat beneath outdoor tents set up close to the banks of the Nile, which provided the necessary supply of water. The result of their labors (below) was a recognizably human form that was believed to guarantee eternal life. (Opposite) This mummy mask was painted gold to mimic the golden skin of the sun god, Re.

characteristics: They were laid flat, with their hands stretched out beside the body; swaddled in fine linen; sculpted with plaster; and then carefully painted. Sometimes even the toes and fingers were individually wrapped. To quote a recent history of mummification, the result was "a virtual linen statue that would serve as a house for the *ka*, or double, of the deceased." Within the wrappings, however, the body often decayed and disintegrated.

During the Middle Kingdom, mummification began to spread to the upper middle classes, which had burgeoned as a result of the increasingly complex nature of the government and religious bureaucracies. At the same time, the embalmers experimented with various improved methods of preserving the body. Evisceration, which became more widespread, was performed both through a slit in the abdominal wall and via the anus, by means of an enema that probably resembled turpentine — the latter method yielding only partial success. Occasionally, Middle Kingdom embalmers removed the brain — usually through the nose, by breaking the ethmoid bone. Natron became the standard method for drying out the body, but embalmers experimented with an additional preservative technique, coating the wrappings with resin made from the sap of various conifers. This resin was later mistaken for bitumen, or *mumia*.

As the body became better preserved, the manner of its wrapping and the nature of its external trappings evolved. The Middle Kingdom brought the first appearance of the painted cartonnage mask — a new way of giving the mummy a lifelike appearance. A few Middle Kingdom mummies have been found with the arms crossed right over left and with the hands placed flat on the chest in what has come to be seen as the classic mummy pose — which imitates most representations of the risen Osiris. But this practice did not become standard, and then only for royal males, until the New Kingdom (18th to 20th Dynasties, 1567-1085 B.C.E.).

The headdress of this queen from the Middle Kingdom takes the form of the protective wings of the vulture goddess Nekhbet, a deity closely associated with Egyptian royalty.

The revival of Egyptian wealth and power during the 18th and 19th Dynasties of the New Kingdom meant that more and more people could afford to be embalmed. This was the classic era of mummification, variants of which continued until the practice began its long decline following the 21st Dynasty (ca. 1089-945 B.C.E.). There were royal and non-royal mummies during the New Kingdom — the only difference between them being the position of the hands. Otherwise, the embalmers followed the same elaborate process to prepare the body for its voyage to the underworld — whether it was a royal one or not.

During the New Kingdom, the internal organs, with the exception of the heart and kidneys, were always removed through a slit in the left side of the lower abdomen, and the brain was extracted through a hole in the nose. If the ancient Egyptians had had any inkling that the brain was the seat of reason and emotion, they might have been more careful to preserve it. However, they thought reason and emotion were seated in the heart. So the brain received no special attention, and by the time it had been extracted, it had become a sort of soupy oatmeal.

This highly stylized tomb scene can be read two ways. In mythological terms, it shows Anubis, the god of embalming, attending the mummy. In human terms, it shows the art of embalming as practiced by a chief embalmer, "the overseer of mysteries," wearing a jackal mask. The elaborately patterned area occupying the upper third of the picture represents a fine embalming tent. The men who oversaw the ritual preparation of the body for the afterlife held priestly titles and conducted themselves according to rituals dating back to the Old Kingdom. Most of the dirty work of eviscerating the corpse and bandaging it for burial was performed by lesser workers.

The four main viscera — the liver, the stomach, the lungs, and the intestines — were dried with natron, then placed in four canopic jars, each representing one of the sons of Horus, the offspring of Osiris. Meanwhile, the body cavities were washed with palm wine, then packed with natron, and the body was covered with natron crystals. Once the process of desiccation was complete — the standard was 40 days after death — the embalmers generally filled the empty spaces in the body with packing material or resin or both. Next came the elaborate process of shrouding the body: the fingers and toes were individually wrapped, then layer after layer of linen was wound around the limbs and the torso. Within the body wrappings, the embalmers often included sacred amulets bearing spells and incantations that were thought to have the effect of speeding the way to the next world. Finally, they applied a generous coat of resin to the wrapped corpse.

The bronze ceremonial embalming knife (top) carries a small figure of Anubis, the jackal god believed to oversee the preparation of the body for burial. (Above) Four canopic jars from the 30th Dynasty tomb of Djedbastefankh. Since earlier times, the jars, each representing one of the four sons of the god Horus, held the four main organs removed from the body. The falcon-headed Qebehsenuef guarded the intestines; the ape-headed Hapy looked after the lungs; the jackal-headed Duamutef held the stomach; and the human-headed Imsety kept the liver. (Right) Auguste Mariette's workers found this remarkable wooden statue of the 5th Dynasty lector-priest Ka-aper in a mastaba tomb near Saqqara. Its haunting eyes were fashioned from rock crystal and set in copper frames.

ACCESSORIES FOR THE AFTERLIFE

Those who could afford it made sure their journey to the next world was well supplied and gorgeously ornamented. Psusennes I wore these gold finger stalls (bottom right) beneath his wrappings and Shoshenq II these gold sandals (bottom left). The scarab pectoral (right) is one of the treasures of King Tutankhamen's tomb. The winged beetle represents the sun, which propels a boat holding the protective eye of Horus, as well as a lunar disk and crescent, representing the phases of the moon.

Tombs could contain as many as several hundred tiny mummiform figures called *ushabtis* or *shabtis*. These statuettes, sometimes equipped with hoes and baskets, and occasionally accompanied by an overseer figure with a whip, were meant to do any menial work the deceased might be called upon to perform in the next world. Usually these figures were inscribed with a text from the *Book of the Dead* as follows: "O ushabti, if [name of deceased] be summoned to do any work which has to be done in the realm of the dead — to make arable the fields, to irrigate the land or to convey sand from east to west; 'Here am I,' you shall say, 'I shall do it.'" Most *ushabtis* are mummiform figures, but during the New Kingdom they occasionally took on ordinary human garb. The blue faïence *ushabtis* (opposite) date from the Late Period (525-332 B.C.E.).

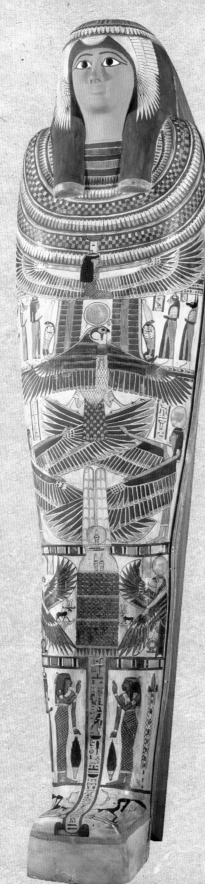

The mummy was then encased in a wooden or cartonnage body coffin, an anthropoid skin reminiscent of the elaborately painted "linen statues" of the Old Kingdom (ca. 2686-2181 B.C.E.). This artificial skin was painted with a stylized likeness of the deceased and decorated with standard inscriptions and ritual scenes, some of which took the form of protective spells to make easier the journey to come. Usually the names of the deceased and the deceased's mother were included.

As the New Kingdom progressed, additions and variants entered the process. Ramesses IV, for example, had onions (a natural antiseptic) placed in his eye sockets and his ears, and a piece of onion skin covered with resin was inserted in each nostril. All sorts of stuffings for the body cavity were also tried, ranging from linen to lichen.

The art of mummification reached its zenith at the beginning of the Third Intermediate Period (21st to 26th Dynasties, 1089-525 B.C.E.). One theory has it that this happened in response to the discovery of pillaged tombs, damaged mummies, and smashed canopic jars from earlier eras. The priests and embalmers of the later time set themselves the task of improving on the work of earlier

A selection of mummy cases and mummy masks from various periods in Egyptian history shows that these works could be as unique as the individuals they contained. Common to all, however, are the representations of elaborate wigs and the detailed inscriptions and decorations that both described and guaranteed the passage of the deceased to the afterlife.

practitioners. By the 21st Dynasty (ca. 1089-945 B.C.E.) they had succeeded.

Never was the embalming process more elaborate, nor its results more lifelike. After preservation with natron, the viscera were packaged and replaced inside the body, although dummy canopic jars sometimes accompanied the burial. Then the body's interior spaces were packed with stuffing, usually a mixture of sawdust and mud, a kind of ancient adobe, which hardened to maintain the body's shape.

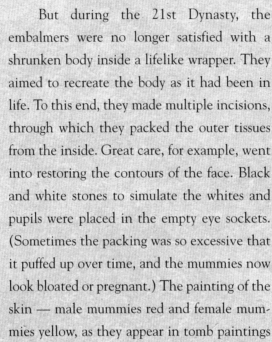

But during the 21st Dynasty, the embalmers were no longer satisfied with a shrunken body inside a lifelike wrapper. They aimed to recreate the body as it had been in life. To this end, they made multiple incisions, through which they packed the outer tissues from the inside. Great care, for example, went into restoring the contours of the face. Black and white stones to simulate the whites and pupils were placed in the empty eye sockets. (Sometimes the packing was so excessive that it puffed up over time, and the mummies now look bloated or pregnant.) The painting of the skin — male mummies red and female mummies yellow, as they appear in tomb paintings — may render the mummy less lifelike to the modern eye, but was meant to depict the tanned skin of men, who mostly worked outside, and the paler skin of women. The final touch of verisimilitude came with the elaborate cosmetic detailing of the face and a fine coiffure. Hair was often dyed back to its youthful color and made thicker with extensions woven onto the existing strands.

(Above) A fine cartonnage mask shows the skill of Late Period craftsmen. (Opposite) Though the two died years apart, this mural from the tomb of 18th-Dynasty Theban sculptors Nebamun and Ipuky shows both men's funerals as if taking place simultaneously. In a further compression of time, the twice-widowed Henutnefret appears for the first time as a young girl at the feet of Ipuky, right, then as an older woman, left, mourning Nebamun.

At their best, the 21st-Dynasty embalmers have never been equaled.

The rest of the story of mummification is one of gradual decline, with occasional highlights, until the practice died out following the introduction of Christianity. During the Greco-Roman period (332 B.C.E.-ca. 600 C.E.), for example, mummies were often wrapped in a splendidly geometric pattern of bandages. Many Greco-Roman mummies from the 1st century C.E. are accompanied by fine portraits of the deceased painted on wooden panels inserted into the cartonnage head cover or surrounding bandages. These are among the earliest surviving painted portraits in the history of art. Over time, however, less and less care went into the embalming process, and the circumstances of burial became simpler and simpler. By sometime during the 6th century C.E., the practice of mummification seems to have died out altogether.

Egyptologists are still adding details to our understanding of how mummification evolved over its more than three-thousand-year history, but they now know enough to be able to date most mummies simply by examining their method of mummification — information of enormous use to modern practitioners of mummy science.

The last days of mummification, when Egypt belonged to the Roman Empire, saw a fascinating cross-fertilization of Egyptian and Greco-Roman styles. Actual portraits of the deceased (below) and in some cases a raised portrait bust (right) replaced the generic cartonnage mask.

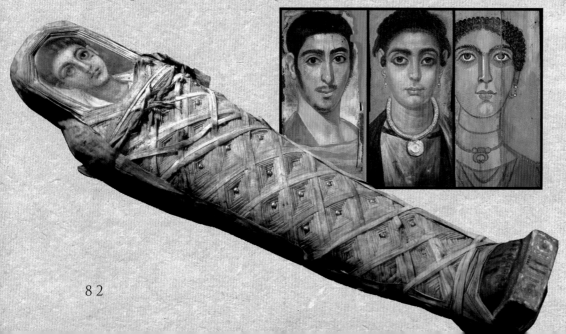

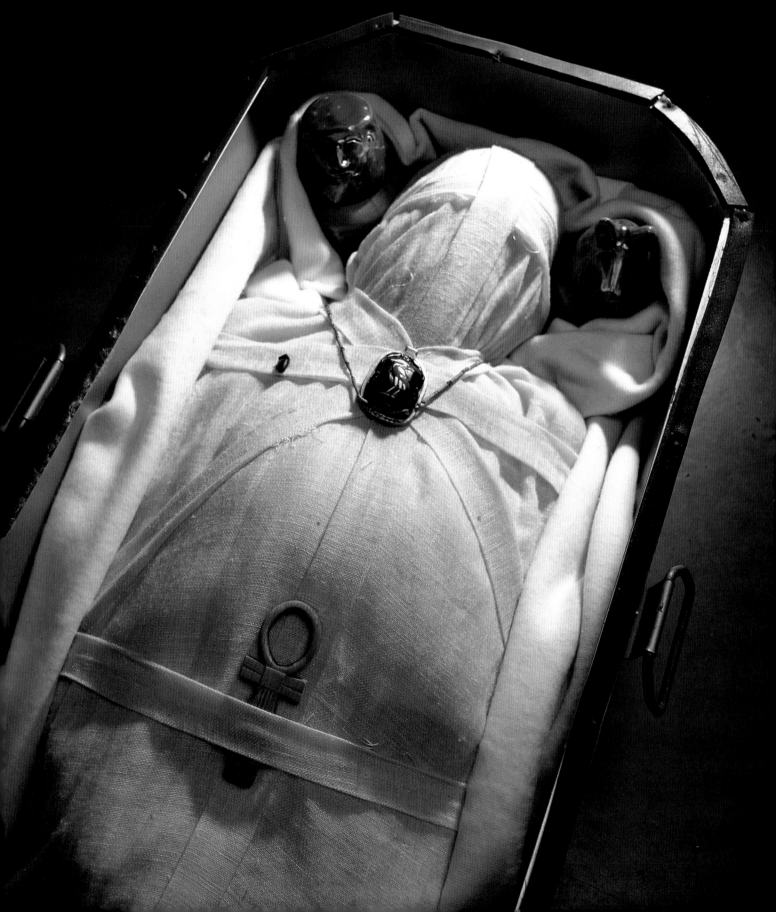

MAKING A MODERN MUMMY

From surviving literature, we know only the broad outline of the ancient Egyptian mummification process. The time from death to entombment was 70 days, during which the body was embalmed, wrapped in linen, and dressed in finery. To better understand the process, Bob Brier (above right), a professor of philosophy and Egyptology, and Ronn Wade (above left), director of the Maryland State Anatomy Board, conducted the first fully documented modern attempt at Egyptian-style mummification (opposite). Brier and Wade's subject was an anonymous 76-year-old man who'd died of a heart attack.

According to the most famous account of the ancient practice, written by the Greek historian Herodotus around 450 B.C.E., the embalmers "first draw out part of the brain through the nostrils with an iron hook . . . . Then, making a cut near the flank with a sharp knife of Etheopean [sic] stone, they take out all the intestines . . . ."

The physical evidence from actual mummies confirms that the brain was removed by puncturing the ethmoid bone in the nose. But in earlier experiments, Brier and Wade had found that the thin metal hook Herodotus described could draw out only a small amount of tissue. Instead, they used the hook like a whisk, stirring the brain until it liquefied. They then placed the cadaver face down on a slight incline and "poured" the brain out through the nose.

Their second challenge was the removal of the viscera. Beyond the point of entry, Brier and Wade knew nothing of how this might have been accomplished. Herodotus's "Etheopean knife" (one with an obsidian blade) was assumed to have had a ritual, not a practical, purpose. Wade made his first attempt at an incision, therefore, with a replica of a copper-bladed tool. It wasn't sharp enough to be effective. The obsidian, however, cut beautifully.

Once all the organs, save the heart, had been removed, Brier and Wade covered the body with natron powder, leaving it to desiccate for 35 days in a room maintained at a dry and suitably Egyptian 90 to 107 degrees Fahrenheit.

(Above) Bob Brier collects natron on a visit to Egypt. (Below) Careful replicas of ancient instruments; the obsidian knife is at far left. Opposite page: The modern embalmers had to lengthen the incision slit slightly to

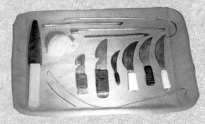

remove the kidneys (top left), the largest organ, raising the possibility that the ancient embalmers cut them in half before removal. (Top center) Following evisceration, the body was covered with 580 pounds of powdered natron. (Top right) After the prescribed 35 days, the natron is removed, exposing a mummy remarkably similar in appearance to its three-thousand-year-old predecessors. (Bottom) The mummy has been carefully wrapped in linen bandages.

When they returned to the embalming room a little more than a month later, they got a surprise: "The skin on the arms and legs of the mummy was still somewhat supple, though leathery, and the limbs could still be flexed." The body had lost half its weight but hadn't yet fully dried out. What to do? Should they repack it with natron or simply leave it exposed as the ancient Egyptians apparently had done?

They chose the latter course. When it came time to wrap the body, it had become completely mummified, showing no signs of putrefaction. Now the Egyptian timetable made more sense: After 35 days, the body is still supple enough to arrange the limbs in the proper burial position. With the body fully mummified, the crossed arms wouldn't stay in place.

Brier and Wade's modern mummy now rests in its temperature-controlled "tomb" three doors away from Ronn Wade's Baltimore office. From time to time, the body is removed for a CAT scan to monitor its state of decay. So far, it has held up very nicely. In all physical respects, this modern mummy is as perfect a candidate for the next world as any mummy made in ancient times.

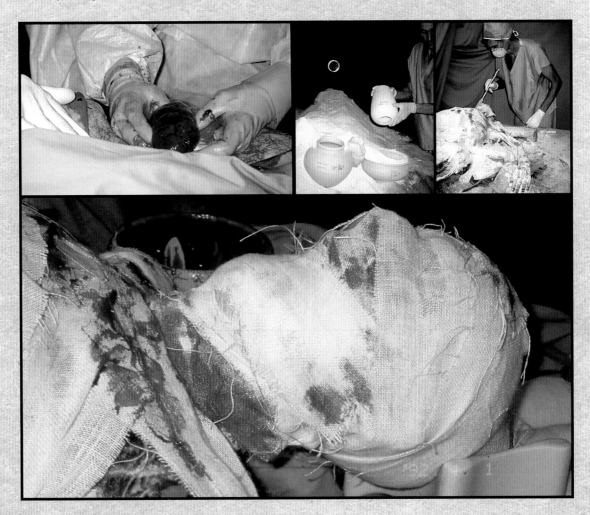

North America's first modern mummy autopsy took place in the basement of the Detroit Institute of Arts, whose Egyptian treasures include the arresting head of a man (above), dating from the Ptolemaic Period (3rd to 2nd century B.C.E.), and an elegant statue of a seated scribe, dating from the New Kingdom, circa 1350 B.C.E.

CHAPTER THREE

NAKHT'S BRAIN

B Y JUNE 1975, WHEN ROSALIE DAVID AND HER BRITISH TEAM PERFORMED THE AUTOPSY ON Mummy 1770 in Manchester, the notion of examining mummies using modern medical science had already taken root on the opposite side of the Atlantic. In the early 1970s, a series of autopsies had been performed on mummies in North American collections, the primary impetus for these coming from Aidan Cockburn, a British-born expert in the evolution of epidemic diseases, who was then supervising a number of medical and dental clinics for the city of Detroit, Michigan. If any one person can be seen as the midwife of modern paleopathology, that person would be Cockburn.

According to Aidan's wife, Eve, who had worked closely with him since their marriage in 1945, the idea of cutting up an ancient body for the sake of science arose from a chance encounter at a scientific convention — the annual gathering of the American Association of Physical Anthropologists in Boston in the early 1970s. While there, Aidan ran into Lucile St. Hoyme, a curator in the Anthropology Department at the National Museum of Natural History in Washington, D.C. St. Hoyme was well acquainted with Dr. Cockburn's theories about when and why certain epidemic diseases recur in certain populations. "Instead of theorizing about where diseases come from and how they evolve," she suggested, "why not test out your ideas?" "How?" he responded. "By studying the evidence of disease in Egyptian mummies."

The Smithsonian Institution could get him a grant that would pay for a reconnaissance trip to Egypt, she added, and would welcome Cockburn as a research associate in the Department of Anthropology. For someone with a lifelong fascination with how diseases got started and how they changed over time, the proposal was irresistible. Very little was known about this subject in the early 1970s. No one then had any inkling that diseases evolve as rapidly as we now know they do.

Back in Detroit, William Peck, the curator of ancient art at the Detroit Institute of Arts, caught wind of Cockburn's plans and approached him with a proposal. In one of the museum's storage rooms resided an Egyptian mummy. Would Aidan like to use it as a test autopsy subject? Cockburn had never performed an autopsy, but he didn't hesitate. How could a scientist refuse such an offer?

A few days later, a small group of pioneers gathered in a basement room of the museum, where the mummy had been laid out on a table. Joining Aidan, his wife Eve, and William Peck were Robin Barraco, a physiologist at Wayne State University's Medical School, and Theodore Reyman, then a senior pathologist at Hutzel Hospital, another part of the Wayne State medical complex. Both Eve Cockburn and Theodore Reyman remember the scene with some amusement. The slightly

(Left) Aidan Cockburn, his ever-present cigar in hand, stands beside PUM-II. (Right) PUM-II and four mummy science pioneers. Left to right: Robin Barraco, Eve Cockburn, Aidan Cockburn, and Theodore Reyman.

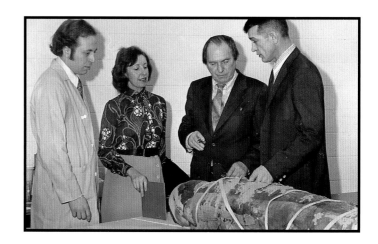

illicit atmosphere of the event was enhanced, says Reyman, by the "very dim lighting" of the basement — all in all, very appropriately cryptlike.

"We just stood around and looked at this corpse," Eve recalls. "None of us had a clue what to do." After an awkward pause, someone — probably William Peck — finally said, "Well, aren't you going to do something?"

Aidan, no surgeon by training, had brought along a set of surgical instruments given him by his favorite professor at the University of Durham. According to legend, they had last seen service at the Battle of Jutland in 1916, where they had been used to remove a ruptured appendix from the Duke of York, later King George VI, a naval officer during World War I.

Finally, Aidan stepped forward and probed through a hole into the chest cavity. (The mummy was in a very poor state. It had been unwrapped many years before, and the hole in the chest was evidence of its dilapidated state.) Not much could be accomplished through such a small opening, however, so Aidan pulled out the surgical saw and offered it to William Peck, who with shaking hands, made the first cut. Then Aidan continued the work of opening the mummy's abdomen. He removed two globular packages — on later analysis these turned out to be wads of resin-soaked linen — and Theodore Reyman took small tissue samples for study back to his hospital laboratory.

Unfortunately, Aidan, who died in 1981, isn't around to tell us what he thought and felt as he made his first incisions into ancient tissue. Given his well-documented ability to make fun of himself and others, however, it seems likely he would have mocked this clumsy maiden attempt. No doubt he would have made the most of the story's punch line: the discovery inside the mummy of a fragment of paper covered with strange hieroglyphs — surely a piece of priceless ancient papyrus? Closer examination revealed this precious artifact to be a set of tide tables for somewhere on the south coast of England dating from the 1800s. Apparently, the current team was not the first to examine this ancient body.

What did the pioneers learn from their hasty and ill-conceived first attempt at a mummy autopsy? "That we didn't have the first idea what we were doing," says Reyman, "and that we'd better do some homework quick." Nonetheless, the experience encouraged the explorers to continue.

THE NEXT TEST TOOK PLACE NOT IN CAIRO BUT IN PHILADELPHIA. SOON AFTER THE DETROIT experiment, Aidan made his planned exploratory trip to Egypt, met with the appropriate authorities, and arranged to return with his autopsy team. While there, he met David O'Connor, then a curator of Egyptology at the Pennsylvania University Museum. When the Egyptian deal unexpectedly fell through, O'Connor invited Cockburn to use a Philadelphia mummy instead.

In May 1972, a mummy designated Pennsylvania University Museum I, or PUM-I, was wheeled into a makeshift operating theater at the Pennsylvania University Museum. Two members of the original Detroit team — Cockburn and Reyman — were joined by Philadelphia pathologist Michael Zimmerman. This time, the autopsy team thought they were much better prepared.

Unknown to the scientists, however, the museum's Public Relations Department, sensing a great opportunity to attract attention to their institution, had issued a press release and invited the media. The room where the autopsy was to take place was barely big enough for the autopsy team, let alone the reporters. As Eve Cockburn remembered it, "the examination became a three-ring circus, with photographers and cameramen taking over the autopsy room." Theodore Reyman recalls there were so many media people present that the autopsy team had trouble getting at the mummy — the TV guys were telling the scientists where to stand for the best camera shots — and that it was almost impossible to work. Adding to the problems, the mummy was in very bad shape, on the verge of crumbling into a heap of dust and a jumble of loose bones.

According to Eve Cockburn, the "circus" reached its absurd peak with the arrival of "a class of visiting third graders, complete with teachers, wandering through and getting underfoot. Not an atmosphere conducive to serious scientific work!" As Rosalie David would learn a couple of years later, the challenge when unwrapping a mummy is not trying to garner publicity, but preventing it from getting out of hand. On top of all this, the mummy proved not to have been embalmed! It was simply a badly decayed body wrapped in some linen cloth. The autopsy had to be rated "an unmitigated disaster."

After this false start in Philadelphia, the Cockburns went home to Detroit to plan a much more ambitious and professional experiment on their own turf. "We certainly realized that we needed to have a lot more control over the proceedings!" says Reyman. Once again, David O'Connor donated a mummy from the Pennsylvania University Museum, PUM-II. Like PUM-I, this was a mummy without an address — its provenance and the manner of its discovery unknown — so once the mummy was safely in their hands, the Detroit pioneers planned to leave nothing to chance.

Eve and Aidan spent months putting together their autopsy team, drawing on the Smithsonian Institution, the Detroit Institute of Arts, and the Wayne State University Medical School, among many sources. As ever, Eve Cockburn seems to have functioned as her husband's perfect complement, devoted to his work but always very much her own woman. Her degree in Modern and Medieval Languages from Oxford gave her a writer's hand and an editor's eye, a distinct analytical perspective on her husband's "sometimes chaotic ideas," and an ability to bridge disparate disciplines with relative ease. Undoubtedly it was her brainwave to make the autopsy the centerpiece of a symposium on "Death and Disease in Ancient Egypt," thus attracting scientists and Egyptologists from Europe and Canada. One of these was a pediatrician from Toronto named Peter Lewin.

Lewin knew more than most people about the diseases suffered by the modern Egyptians. His father, a physician with the Royal Army Medical Corps stationed in Alexandria from 1939 to 1956, had treated ailments ranging from malaria to ophthalmia militensis. Lewin grew up in the city immortalized by Lawrence Durrell in his *Alexandria Quartet*, a modern cosmopolitan place with ancient roots. (The tomb of Alexander the Great may lie somewhere beneath its streets.) One of Lewin's high school classmates at the elite Victoria College was the future King Hussein of Jordan. But above all, he remembers the family outings to ancient sites, many of them out of the way, some of them on military property. It was on these excursions that Lewin became a keen amateur archeologist.

In 1973, Lewin was a staff physician at Toronto's renowned Hospital for Sick Children, but he still had Egypt in his bones, and he'd been dabbling in what he liked to call "medical archeology" since 1966. That year, the curator of the Near Eastern Department at Toronto's Royal Ontario Museum had presented him with a mummified hand dating from around 600 B.C.E. Lewin was able to soften up a fragment of skin tissue using Ruffer's Solution, then slice it thinly enough to study it under an electron microscope. "To my absolute amazement, I could see intact skin cells, beautifully preserved," he remembers. "It was one of the most exciting moments in my life."

Some of the cells contained intact organelles, the specialized structures that allow a living cell to function. This discovery raised the possibility that ancient proteins might have survived, and with them, genetic information. If human cells remained intact for three thousand years, ancient microbes and their antibodies might still exist in mummy tissue. More mummies would have to be studied, however, before the Holy Grail of paleopathology was likely to be found: an intact virus or bacterium. Perhaps this prize would be discovered within the ancient tissue of PUM-II.

Robin Barraco and a fellow scientist lean forward to examine the hole made in the abdomen of PUM-II. Just getting to this stage took eight hours.

NO ONE PRESENT THAT FEBRUARY DAY IN 1973 IN THE WELL-EQUIPPED dissecting room at Wayne State University Medical School in Detroit would forget the intense spicy smell that filled the room as the Stryker saw slowly cut through PUM-II's rocklike wrappings, giving off a pungent smoke. As was common with mummies from the New Kingdom (1567-1085 B.C.E.) onward, the bandages had been soaked in resin, which gradually dried and solidified. For eight hours, the team used hammers and chisels, as well as the surgical saw, to chip away the mummy's seal without damaging the body within. Finally, all 12 layers of bandages were removed and the real autopsy could begin.

"Each new revelation confirmed that this mummy was indeed a treasure," wrote Eve Cockburn in a published account of the unwrapping. "The fingernails and toenails were intact and stained reddish with henna. The soles of the feet had been painted white. Eyelashes were still in position, and whiskers on the chin were clearly visible. The arms, crossed over the breast in traditional style, added to the total impression of a serene personality, who seemed to reach across the ages to these 20th-century scientists."

To the surprise of the radiologists present, who had concluded from the preliminary X-rays that PUM-II was female, the mummy possessed a three-inch penis. (The Egyptians often embalmed and wrapped the penis separately, apparently honoring its role in procreation.) As was often the case, however, the testicles had been removed. The abdominal cavity also contained several packages of internal organs — a wealth of material for future study.

J. Lawrence Angel, the Smithsonian Institution's curator of physical anthropology, measured the bones and concluded the age of death was between 34 and 40. Eugen Strouhal, a physician and anthropologist from Prague, weighed the cultural evidence — the position of the arms, the painted nails, the manner of wrapping, the placement of the wrapped organs inside the body rather than in separate canopic jars — and dated the mummy from about 700 B.C.E.

As each painstaking hour passed, PUM-II emerged from beneath his rocklike wrappings (above right) to reveal his remarkably lifelike remains, including a beautifully preserved hand (left). Once the resin-soaked bandages had been chipped away from the upper face, fragments of eyelashes were found in place, but these disappeared during cleaning (above left). The body proved to be in classic position (below), with its arms crossed upon its chest.

Any tentative conclusions about the cause of death would have to wait for subsequent laboratory analysis, but one immediate finding intrigued and puzzled the participants and created quite a buzz at the symposium that took place the day following the autopsy. Among PUM-II's wrappings, the autopsy team discovered a small ball of cotton, a tiny clue with sweeping implications.

According to conventional belief, cotton did not show up in the Mediterranean world until around the time of Christ. Did its presence in the wrappings mean the Egyptians had cultivated cotton hundreds of years earlier? Or did it imply trade with one of the places where cotton was definitely grown in PUM-II's time — India or South America? Either conclusion meant rewriting Egyptian history. It was a forceful reminder of the importance of hard physical evidence in formulating historical hypotheses.

In the ensuing months, PUM-II's shrunken tissues yielded up solid proof of ancient disease. Not surprisingly, given the smoky and ill-ventilated houses in which ancient Egyptians lived, his lungs were full of carbon particles: he had black lung disease. And, like many modern Bedouins, he suffered from sand pneumoconiosis, or desert lung disease. Sand was part of the air the ancient Egyptians breathed. But PUM-II's problems didn't stop in his lungs. He had a parasitic roundworm in his gut and — surprising for one so young — showed clear signs of arteriosclerosis, or hardening of the arteries, a disease generally thought to have been rare in ancient times. And when a specialist in diseases of the ear examined PUM-II's ear canals, he found the earliest ever example of a perforated eardrum, a sure sign that PUM-II had at some point suffered from a severe ear infection. However, as to which of these diseases killed PUM-II, the Detroit team couldn't be sure. Perhaps his ailments combined to weaken him sufficiently that he fell prey to a fatal fever.

The autopsy of PUM-II stands as the first successful modern autopsy of an Egyptian mummy. It also led directly to the founding of the Paleopathology Association, an informal grouping created by Eve and Aidan Cockburn to encourage the interdisciplinary study of ancient diseases — and not only those found among the ancient Egyptians. Soon the association began publishing a quarterly newsletter, edited by Eve. (She only retired from the editorship in 1999.) Its more than one hundred issues and numerous supplements would ultimately chronicle the growth of mummy science and the achievements of mummy scientists around the world, who soon ventured far beyond the boundaries of ancient Egypt.

OTHER ANCIENT PEOPLES PRACTICED MUMMIFICATION, INCLUDING THE INCA AND THE PREHISTORIC inhabitants of the Aleutian Islands and the Canaries. Dry climates such as that of the American Southwest have also preserved ancient bodies, as have extremely cold environments. The Arctic ice has yielded prehistoric human and animal remains, including several intact woolly mammoths; a number of Inca remains have turned up in the high Andes. A prehistoric hunter recently resurfaced in the Alps and another in Canada's Yukon. If the trend toward global warming continues, many more ancient people and animals may be released from the ice. But Egypt offers an unbeatable combination: a potentially inexhaustible number of specimens from a relatively homogeneous population that has not changed radically from ancient times to the present day. Not only is there more evidence available than anywhere else in the world, but this evidence

Nakht's decorated wooden casket is remarkably fine for that of a poor weaver.

is also more likely to provide clues about the history and evolution of diseases that are still around.

PUM-II had given up some of these clues. He had also told us how old he was when he died and roughly when he lived. But he could not tell us his name or where he was born, who his family was or what his social station was. As a body, he made an interesting subject for scientific study. As a human being, he remained a mystery. How much more meaningful his autopsy would have been had Aidan Cockburn and his colleagues been able to place him more precisely in his ancient world.

To a professional Egyptologist like Nicholas Millet, the curator of Egyptology at the Royal Ontario Museum, this was precisely the problem with many early mummy autopsies. As he saw it, the scientists couldn't wait to cut up the mummy and divide up its tissue to take it back to their labs and put it under their microscopes. They didn't really care who the ancient person was. As Millet puts it now, "It didn't make much sense to me and probably wouldn't have made much sense to any serious Egyptologist to autopsy a mummy unless you could firmly place him in his historical context."

Presumably, the ROM curator made this very point to Eve and Aidan Cockburn following Aidan's lecture about the autopsy of PUM-II, which he delivered at the Toronto Academy of Medicine in February 1974. The following day, Eve proposed a joint Canadian-American autopsy, to take place in Toronto. The day after that, Nicholas Millet offered a mummy from the museum collection. He believed he had the perfect candidate, one that would please both the Egyptologists and the scientists.

The mummy in question resided in a simple wooden coffin stashed in the museum's basement storeroom. It had been brought back from Egypt at the beginning of the 20th century by the Royal Ontario Museum's first director, Charles T. Currelly, who had spent many years excavating in the valley of the Nile. Unlike the case for so many mummies, Millet knew exactly where both the coffin and the simply wrapped body inside it had come from. Better still, the hieroglyphic inscription on the coffin dated it quite precisely to early in the 20th Dynasty in the New Kingdom, a period better documented than most. Best of all, it identified the mummy as a Theban weaver named Nakht, who had worked at the temple of King Sethnakhte, the dynasty's founder. Since the coffin lid was easily removed, it would suffer no damage if Nakht went under the surgeon's scalpel.

No one seemed to mind that Nakht wasn't really a mummy, at least not in the classic sense. Preliminary X-rays showed his internal organs were all in place, which meant he had not been embalmed according to the standard New Kingdom process but simply wrapped and placed in his coffin. The dry Egyptian climate had done the rest. This fact was not surprising for a poorly paid weaver, since mummification was very expensive. It was quite surprising that such a lowly fellow had been given such a proper burial. An intact body made the scientists even more eager to begin work because there was more tissue for them to study.

The X-rays had other stories to tell. Nakht's bone development was that of someone whose body was still growing: he was probably a young teenager. Telltale lines on his shin bones hinted at malnutrition or possibly a prolonged illness with high fever. These stress lines are markers of arrested growth. We all have them, since they occur whenever we become ill and our growth temporarily slows. But Nakht's stress lines were more frequent and more visible than normal. Apparently food was scarce in Thebes early in the 20th Dynasty.

One of the keenest members of the impressive team gathered in Room 1128 of the Anatomy Building of the Medical Science Complex at the University of Toronto on Friday, August 9, 1974, was a young Torontonian named Patrick Horne. Ordinarily, Horne would have been stationed in his laboratory at the Banting Institute, where he worked as part of the Toronto General Hospital's Department of Pathology, spending long hours peering at human cells through an electron microscope and staining tissue samples so they could be examined for evidence of disease in living patients. But his real passion was mummy science.

After graduating from the University of Toronto in 1969, Horne spent several months in Chile and Peru as a member of Canadian University Services Overseas (CUSO), a Canadian version of the Peace Corps. At the time, there were only two electron microscopes in South America, and he traveled with one of them, teaching local pathologists the art of modern medical histology — the microscopic examination of body tissue. While journeying through Chile's high and dry Atacama Desert — one of the driest climates on the planet — he began noticing that "there were mummies everywhere." These were the naturally mummified remains of the pre-Columbian inhabitants of this remote region, which may house the greatest concentration of natural mummies in the world. The more he traveled through this amazing landscape, the more Horne asked himself, "Why don't I take what I know about pathology and apply it to mummies?"

Back in Toronto, he presented himself at Nicholas Millet's office in the Royal Ontario Museum and asked the curator if he would lend him a piece of a mummy to put under his microscope. Millet, who doesn't suffer fools gladly, sent the long-haired young man away without encouragement. "He probably thought I was some crazy hippie," Horne says now. Undeterred, Horne did some research and knocked on Millet's door again. And again. Finally, the curator decided that the young histologist was serious and lent him a slice from one of the mummy pieces in his storeroom. Horne studied it in his spare time, then wrote a brief scholarly paper on what he found. That's how he came to the attention of Aidan Cockburn, who invited him to participate in the autopsy of PUM-II. Horne then worked closely with Peter Lewin and the Toronto team organizing the autopsy of Nakht, the Weaver.

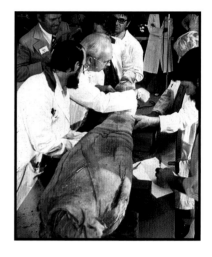

(Above) Nakht's autopsy begins in a dissection room in the University of Toronto's Department of Anatomy. (Opposite) The fully unwrapped body of Nakht lies on the dissecting table. His badly damaged skull was later reconstructed.

The Toronto autopsy combined a local group of specialists with the veterans of Detroit, and Egyptologists from both countries provided expert support. The co-chairmen of the autopsy were Aidan Cockburn and Gerald Hart, a noted Toronto hematologist. Peter Lewin, Theodore Reyman (of Hutzel Hospital, Detroit), and Michael Zimmerman (of Lankenau Hospital, Philadelphia) headed the core team of doctors assisting at the autopsy, which had been planned with military precision.

However, as Patrick Horne remembers, no amount of planning could take into account every eventuality. As the first day of the two-day autopsy was about to begin, it suddenly became apparent that despite months of planning meetings, no one had solved the problem of how to weigh a mummy. Nakht was as stiff as a board but extremely fragile. He couldn't just be popped on a scale. Finally, Michael Zimmerman, volunteered his wife Bobbie as the solution. The petite Bobbie agreed to hold the even more diminutive mummy gently in her arms, then step on the scale. When her weight was subtracted from the total, voilà! — the weight of a mummy. Nakht tipped the scales at 5.13 kilograms, a mere 11.3 pounds.

The first day was devoted to unwrapping the mummy, a task performed by Nicholas Millet and a group of colleagues from the Royal Ontario Museum. In contrast to PUM-II's rocklike bandages, Nakht's came away easily, not having been soaked in resin — an expense his family had clearly been unable to afford. The unwrappers simply rolled up each long strip of cream-colored linen — perhaps once used as bed sheets — the fabric of which proved to be exceptionally well preserved. A few

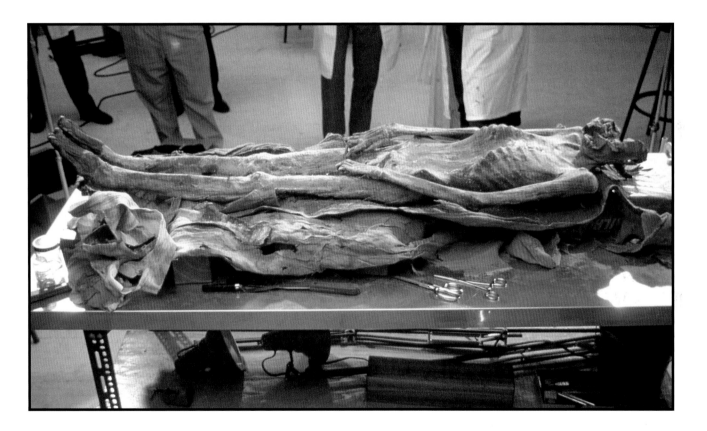

pieces, stitched with blue borders, seemed to have been included for their greater tensile strength. These and other wrappings were laid aside. More detailed analysis could wait for later.

Once the torso had been laid bare, Millet and his confreres made a wonderful discovery: The concave depression in Nakht's shrunken abdomen had been filled out with two shirts, sleeveless tunics of the sort the weaver undoubtedly wore and that were probably part of his personal wardrobe. More wonderful still, the tunics would join the ROM's Textile Department as the oldest hemmed garments in its collection.

The cadaver that now lay exposed on the autopsy table appeared to be in reasonably good shape for a body that had already lasted three thousand years. For the most part, its skin was intact and possessed of a tough, leathery consistency. Nakht's face had been shaved before burial, and his nails had been trimmed. (His toenails were in excellent condition.) Disappointingly, his skull was badly damaged, and most of the facial bones had collapsed into the cranial cavity. Lastly, as if to emphasize the poor weaver's connection to his 20th-century descendants, one foot bore a nicely developed plantar wart.

On the second day, the autopsy proper commenced. Here it seems appropriate to pause and consider the remarkable progress of mummy science in the few short years since that first faltering autopsy attempt in the ill-lit basement of the Detroit Institute of Arts. The scholars and scientists gathered that August day in the air-conditioned autopsy room in the Anatomy Department of the Medical Sciences Building on the campus of the University of Toronto made up an impressive international and intellectual assembly. Joining the American pioneers — the Cockburns, Reyman, Barraco, and Zimmerman — and the ROM Egyptologists, was the distinguished team of Toronto medical scientists brought together by Dr. Gerald Hart, head of the Haematology Department at Toronto East General Hospital and chairman of the Museum Committee of the Toronto Academy of Medicine.

Dr. David Rideout, director of diagnostic radiology at Princess Margaret Hospital, took charge of the pre-autopsy X-rays. Dr. John Scott, professor of physiology at the University of Toronto, who had persuaded his colleagues Dr. Jim Thompson and Dr. Ross MacKenzie to provide autopsy space in the university's Anatomy Department, supervised specimen collection. (Dr. Thompson, as the only specialist in anatomy present that day, guided the dissectors through the often-confusing territory of Nakht's remains.) Dr. Peter Lewin, staff physician at the Hospital for Sick Children, led the dissection team. Patrick Horne, technologist in charge in the Department of Pathology of Toronto General Hospital, oversaw specimen storage and distribution and took particular responsibility for post-autopsy microscopic studies.

Presiding over the entire event like some guardian angel, as he had over the many months of planning and preparation, was Professor William Swinton, whose résumé read like a novel — on one occasion he had explained the extinction of the dinosaurs to the young princesses Elizabeth and Margaret — and whose career perfectly bridged the many disciplines combined under the umbrella of paleopathology. Swinton had retired as director of the Royal Ontario Museum in 1966, but continued as professor of zoology and Centennial Professor of the History of Science at the University of Toronto. And it appears to have been his reputation, his force of character, and his sense of humor that suited him perfectly to the fatherly role he played. Gerald Hart recalls with

A modern Egyptian weaver about Nakht's age sits at a vertical loom. Unlike Nakht, however, this boy does not squat, but perches on a bench to do his work.

pleasure Swinton's tongue-in-cheek explanation of the proper way to examine a prehistoric skull: "You sit down with the skull in the right hand and a gin and tonic in the left. . . ."

On the day in question, however, the gin and tonic had to wait, for a great deal needed to be accomplished in a small timespan. Compared to the two-week autopsy of Mummy 1770 in Manchester the following year, the daylong Toronto autopsy proper may seem to have been a speedy affair, but it was conducted with great care and had to be judged a major success. The team worked

(Left) Peter Lewin and Gerald Hart examine Nakht's brain before removing it from the skull. (Below) The two perfectly preserved hemispheres made Nakht's the oldest intact human brain yet discovered.

without interference from the media, who had to await the press conference at day's end for an autopsy report. A staff photographer from the ROM took still photographs, and a member of the Department of Medical Photography at Toronto East General recorded the event for posterity on 16 mm film.

As Dr. Rideout had so confidently predicted from the X-rays, Nakht's internal organs proved to be in place and for the most part intact, confirming that his body had not been eviscerated. His heart was still attached to the sternum. His liver, though shrunken, was readily identifiable. His kidneys, bladder, and prostate were all in one piece. His bowel had survived but was, in Gerald Hart's words, "as flimsy as tissue paper." In the worst shape were the collapsed lungs and the enlarged spleen, the latter appearing to have ruptured, staining the surrounding abdominal wall with blood.

But the highlight of the day for everyone present seems to have been the recovery of Nakht's brain, which was discovered by Dr. Scott in the course of palpating the contents of the cranial vault. Because the embalming process from the Middle Kingdom onward included the brain's removal, even the more seasoned veterans in the room had never seen an ancient brain before. Nakht's brain — the two hemispheres had separated but were otherwise perfect — was then the oldest intact human brain ever found.

Gently, with an almost religious reverence, the scientists passed the two small black objects, each about one-third its original size, from hand to hand. "They felt like soap," Lewin recalls. Gerald Hart thought they had the consistency of India rubber. The soapy feel comes from adipocere, or "grave wax," caused by a naturally occurring chemical process called hydrolysis, which converts the fat in human tissue into a waxy substance. As Nakht's brain dehydrated in the dry Theban climate, the fat in his brain tissue was converted into grave wax, preserving the brain in the process.

At the end of the long but exhilarating day, Nakht's slight body lay in pieces. Samples of his tissues, including parts of his lungs, liver, kidneys, stomach, intestines, and spleen, had been carefully logged and labeled for future study. That evening, the autopsy participants gathered at Toronto's exclusive Royal Canadian Yacht Club for a celebration dinner, hosted by a genial Professor Swinton. The next day they dispersed, carrying their precious pieces of ancient flesh back to their laboratories, where each would seek evidence of disease, using the techniques and technologies of the seventh decade of the 20th century.

The first and most venerable of these approaches was radiology. Since the pioneering mummy roetgenograms just before and after the turn of the century, thousands more mummies had been X-rayed. (The building of the second Aswan Dam in the 1960s sparked another massive effort to examine every mummy that was about to be inundated.) But by the mid-1970s, the art of the X-ray had become considerably more sophisticated. As well as old-fashioned radiograms, radiologists could make xerograms, which gave a much clearer picture of a body's soft tissue. A preliminary X-ray of the mummy of Nakht had sketched a roadmap for its dissection.

The first level of analysis during and following Nakht's autopsy fell under the general heading of Gross Anatomy. Like Douglas Derry examining the skeleton of Tutankhamen in 1925, the Toronto investigators learned a good deal by simply observing the state of Nakht's body. From the nature of the damage to his skull, they could safely conclude that it had caved in after the burial. The enlarged spleen, which was surrounded by a dark mass, possibly indicating bleeding at the time of death, suggested a diagnosis of malaria. The state of the skeleton pinpointed Nakht's age at about 15 years. Allowing for skeletal shrinkage, his height was 4 feet, 8.25 inches.

ETERNITY FOR EVERYONE

In recent years, mummy scientists have taken their knowledge out into the archeological field. Between 1994 and 1997 a team of French researchers — historian Françoise Dunand; anthropologist Jean-Louis Helm; radiologists Roger and Martine Lichtenberg — conducted a fascinating series of excavations of a Late Period (525-332 B.C.E.) necropolis near the village of Aïn Labakha in the vast Kharga oasis southwest of Luxor. Their detailed analysis of some 60 mummies of ordinary people confirmed that in Roman Egypt the arts of mummification had fil-

tered down to common folk. The Lichtenbergs' X-rays revealed that these had been hard-working people — a number suffered from spinal rheumatism, associated with the carrying of heavy burdens. Four showed clear signs of tuberculosis, and many had died suffering from the endemic parasitic disease schistosomiasis. Many of the women and their infants had died in childbirth.

Such portraits of a population promise to add greatly to our knowledge of the ancient world. Thanks to the advances of paleopathology, we can expect many more of them in the coming years.

(Above left) A chamber in the cliffside necropolis of Douch, about 120 kilometers south of Aïn Labakha. (Top) Françoise Dunand labels mummies that have just been removed from their tomb. (Above) After the mummies had been examined, they were returned to their resting places. (Right) Raïs Saad, leader of the Egyptian team, and Françoise Dunand carry mummies to the bottom of the cliff face.

So far, the 1974 analysis of Nakht could have been reproduced almost entirely by Elliot Smith and his colleagues in Cairo during the century's first decade. For the tissue analysis, however, recent advances in histology came to the fore. When Marc Armand Ruffer pioneered the study of mummy tissue before World War I, he could examine these ancient cells using only a conventional light microscope — but the electron microscopes available to the Toronto autopsy team in 1974 could magnify thousands of times more than Ruffer's. (In a delightful case of historical synchronicity, the electron microscope was first developed in Toronto during the 1930s.)

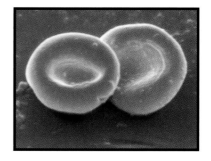

Under the electron microscope, Nakht's three-thousand-year-old blood cells retain their classic circular concave shape.

GERALD HART AND PATRICK HORNE SPENT A GOOD DEAL OF THEIR SPARE time during the months following the autopsy looking at Nakht's blood. For those unfamiliar with the arduous process of basic lab-work, it is difficult to imagine the hours and hours of trials and errors that precede even the least significant discovery. First the tissue must be rehydrated, then sectioned — the thinner the better — then mounted on a slide, then fixed and stained. Only then can it be examined beneath the microscope's magnifying gaze. Horne has lost count of the hundreds of slides he prepared and examined before the payoff.

But one day, he recalls, "I looked in the microscope and found intact red blood cells." This was one of those wonderful moments that makes basic research worthwhile. "I was absolutely shocked and thrilled," he says now, the excitement still evident in his voice. As far as he knew, no one had ever before gazed on ancient blood. He rushed over to the Royal Ontario Museum, which then possessed Toronto's only scanning electron microscope. Unlike the transmission microscope in his lab at the Banting Institute, which sees *through* the tissue, a scanning microscope surveys the surface, shows you the lay of the land. At the ROM, Horne took micrographs of the blood cells, photos that showed their classic shape, "like little concave saucers" resembling donuts from which the hole has been only partly cut.

"At seven o'clock one morning I roared up to Gerald Hart's office and stuck the micrographs under his nose," he continues. "I can still remember the expression on his face. We were so excited we were almost dancing." As it turned out, however, an autopsy colleague beat them to publication. Pathologist Michael Zimmerman had published an article describing his earlier discovery of red blood cells in the pulmonary vein of a naturally mummified two-thousand-year-old American Native person, and the finding had made the cover of *Science*. But Nakht's were still the oldest intact blood cells ever found. And if blood cells had survived, then so might have gamma globulins, the proteins that make up the antibodies the body manufactures to combat infection. A mummy's blood might yield the first hard microscopic evidence of ancient bacteria or viruses. (Horne would later become the first researcher to definitively identify an intact virus in ancient tissue, that of an astonishingly well-preserved Incan teenager known as the Prince of Paloma.)

In recalling Nakht's autopsy and its aftermath, Gerald Hart is at pains to single out the laboratory technologists, like Patrick Horne, whose work is often less well sung than it ought to be. In Hart's laboratory at Toronto East General, he and two colleagues developed a technique for blood typing ancient bones by drawing on modern forensic techniques. After much hard labor, they determined that Nakht's blood belonged to blood group B. "It was an example of the kind of teamwork that comprises much of basic research," he says now. "These scientists often don't get the credit they deserve." And so, for the record, here are the names of Hart's associates: Dr. Marja Soots and Mrs. Inge Kvas.

Like most ancient Egyptian bodies, Nakht's had been invaded by more than one parasite. His included a tapeworm, here seen in microscopic cross-section.

The electron microscope added many details to the emerging picture of Nakht, the Weaver, but did not complete it. Like PUM-II, Nakht had suffered from both black lung disease and desert lung disease. Perhaps these conditions were epidemic in ancient Egypt. A tapeworm and many tapeworm eggs found in Nakht's intestine indicated that the poor weaver had been a meat eater. He was later found to have had trichinosis, the first hard evidence that Egyptians of this era ate pork. These findings surprised the Egyptologists, who had formerly believed that a dietary proscription against pork had been practiced in ancient Egypt.

But the tapeworm was only the beginning of his parasitic complaints. He was also infected with schistosomiasis, a serious health problem in Egypt to this day. The schistosome parasite lays eggs in the bladder and the liver, probably explaining why Nakht suffered from cirrhosis of the liver. A third parasitic infection, malaria, suggested by Nakht's enlarged spleen, was not positively diagnosed until the 1990s. As biohistorian Arno Karlen would later say, Nakht was "a veritable museum of parasitic infections."

The overall picture that emerged from the autopsy was that of a malnourished and disease-ridden teenager, whose brief life cannot have been very pleasant — a far cry from the idealized image of ancient Egyptian life that comes down to us from funerary texts. As for the immediate cause of Nakht's death, it seems to have been pneumonia, which starved his already damaged lungs of oxygen. He probably suffocated to death.

Among the masses of medical evidence accumulated from the autopsy of Nakht, one trifling clue opened a fascinating window into the poor weaver's life story. Many months after the event, a researcher at the University of Cardiff reported that the sand particles in Nakht's lung tissue were composed of red granite. Red granite occurs in only one place in Egypt — Aswan, which is many miles upriver from the town of Thebes, where Nakht had died.

To ROM curator Nicholas Millet, the red granite could mean only one thing: "Clearly, our Nakht had been a bad boy." The granite quarries of Aswan provided the raw material for royal sarcophagi and great public monuments. Huge blocks of the stone were floated on barges down the Nile, then finished under the direction of expert carvers. But the grueling and unhealthy work of dressing the stone for the skilled carvers to finish was meted out as punishment. What had Nakht done to earn this harsh sentence?

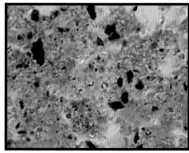

Sand particles in Nakht's lungs (dark spots in picture) are evidence of pulmonary silicosis, a common complaint among desert-dwelling people.

AFTER HIS AUTOPSY, NAKHT WAS DONATED TO TORONTO'S ACADEMY OF Medicine. Among his organs, only the brain and the heart had not been subjected to the surgeon's knife or the histologist's slicing machine. From the outside, Nakht's brain looked perfectly healthy, so there seemed no justification for investigating it and therefore possibly damaging it. For several years it sat, along with Nakht's other organs, in a display case at the Academy that also contained his eviscerated body. The mummy had been glued back together and the dissection lines were clearly visible. But none of those involved in Nakht's autopsy could forget the experience of holding that ancient brain in their hands. If only they could have peered inside it.

Here precisely was the challenge facing paleopathology in 1974 when Nakht was dissected. It was the same challenge faced by Rosalie David and her colleagues in 1975 as they considered the lessons learned from the unwrapping and autopsy of Mummy 1770: How could they achieve equivalent results without harming the mummy? How could they perform a hands-off autopsy that was as good as the real thing? In case they needed to be reminded of their limitations, in the early fall of 1976, Ramesses II flew to Paris.

There is something both comic and touching about the arrival of the remains of the most famous pharaoh of the New Kingdom at Le Bourget Airport on September 26, 1976. When his carefully packed coffin descended from a French military transport, it was accorded the same reception due any visiting head of state. (Rumor has it that his specially issued passport bore the description, "King, Deceased.") And the pomp drew attention to the significance of the event. For Ramesses the Great was the first royal mummy ever permitted to leave Egypt. And the perilous state of his body could not be ascribed to age or decrepitude at the time of his death at the ripe old age of 91, after a reign of

67 years. No, Ramesses was suffering from a very modern problem: air pollution.

Since 1881, when the mummy of Ramesses was discovered with roughly 40 others in the royal cache at Deir el Bahri, it had been affected by modern contamination. First it had been unceremoniously unwrapped by Gaston Maspero, then director of the Antiquities Service at the Cairo Museum. A few years later Elliot Smith had done his own more scientific examination. Neither had been interested in preserving the mummy. Maspero and his VIP audience only wanted to gaze on the face of the famous pharaoh; Smith was primarily interested in the details of his embalming for the book he would write on the history of Egyptian mummification. Neither took any precautions to protect the pharaoh's fragile remains.

For most of this century, Ramesses II had resided in the Mummy Room of the Cairo Museum in a wooden coffin within a glass case, his sunken face still hinting at the willful pride that had ruled an empire, as his body wasted steadily away. His case was neither hermetically sealed nor climate-controlled. When Dr. Maurice Bucaille arrived to examine Ramesses prior to the pharaoh's possible participation in an exhibition in Paris in his honor, the physician found the monarch in a shocking state of decay, being eaten away by the bacteria and fungi that had accompanied the countless visitors to the museum over the years. The Egyptian authorities decided to allow Ramesses to travel to Paris, but for conservation, not display. The long-dead pharaoh was about to undergo an elaborate exercise in mummy renovation.

THE PHARAOH TAKES A TRIP

The arrival of the mummy of Ramesses II in Paris in September 1976 made news around the world. One of the first challenges the French scientists faced was how to remove him from his oak coffin, which had been transported

inside a specially built shipping container (above left). Not that the pharaoh posed a heavy burden: his dried-out body weighed less than 40 pounds. After some debate, the scientists at the Musée de l'Homme decided to saw off the end of the coffin so that a thin sheet of Altuglas (similar to Plexiglas) could be slid under the cloth mattress on which the pharaoh lay. Once the mummy was free of its case, the mattress could be cut away — each piece of cloth would be numbered and sent off for laboratory analysis. Then the process of investigation and conservation could begin. One of the first tasks to complete was a radiological analysis of the pharaoh's skeleton (above right). This suggested that the elderly Ramesses had walked with a slight limp and with his head tilted forward.

THE ROYAL CACHE

The greatest single discovery of royal mummies took place at Deir el Bahri, an ancient funerary site on the west bank of the Nile across from Luxor. Until 1881, it was known above all for the magnificent 18th-Dynasty temple of Queen Hatshepsut, built into the cliffs that border on the nearby Valley of the Kings. But it was also the site of many shaft tombs from the Middle Kingdom. And it was to one of these that local villagers led Émile Brugsch, then the assistant to Gaston Maspero, Egypt's director of antiquities. Inside the tomb Brugsch discovered 40 royal mummies, including pharaohs of the New Kingdom and the later 21st Dynasty. The New Kingdom finds included Ramesses II and his father Sethos I, secretly reburied here during the 21st Dynasty, after their tombs in the Valley of the Kings were robbed. The tomb had actually been discovered by the villagers a decade or so before Brugsch's visit and had provided a steady income in pilfered treasures until then.

For seven months, from September 1976 until May 1977, the remains of Ramesses the Great went through as thorough an analysis, cleaning, and refurbishing as has ever been accorded an ancient body. After being unwrapped, Ramesses received a head-to-toe facelift: every crack in his skin was filled with a compound composed of beeswax, turpentine, and Vaseline. He was X-rayed and photographed from every angle; his hair — dyed red-blond by the embalmers — was analyzed. Not surprisingly, its true color was pure white, but originally it had been red, a color the ancient Egyptians associated with the god Seth. His ancient wrappings were cleaned and then carefully wound around his body once more. Finally, when all human hands had finished their work, he was bombarded with gamma rays, the same process used to sterilize food. By the time Ramesses was ready to make the return trip to Cairo, he looked to be in better shape than he had been in many years — and he was completely sterile. A specially designed two-piece case made of a type of Plexiglas was built to ensure that he would remain so.

During Ramesses' Parisian stay, much had been learned about his final days, primarily from X-rays. A physical autopsy of a royal mummy was out of the question, although the French scientists did make gentle skin scrapings, especially near the evisceration scar, in which they later discovered more than 80 different species of fungi — presumably all post-mortem arrivals. Before his death, the great Ramesses suffered from advanced arteriosclerosis and from a dental abscess so

No Egyptian place name evokes more dramatic associations than the Valley of the Kings. It was here in 1922 that Howard Carter unearthed the tomb of the boy pharaoh Tutankhamen, whose virtually intact burial chamber held unimaginable riches. If a pharaoh so little known and so short lived had been buried in such splendor, what must the tombs of greater pharaohs have contained?

The so-called Valley of the Kings actually consists of two interconnected valleys on the west bank of the Nile about five kilometers west of Luxor where the New Kingdom pharaohs excavated elaborate — and, they hoped, impenetrable — tombs in the cliffs. But of the 62 tombs so far discovered, all, save Tut's, had been completely plundered. We can therefore only guess at the magnificent accoutrements meant to accompany Sethos I or Tuthmosis II into the next world.

But the tombs are treasures in themselves, elaborately decorated and providing important evidence of the evolution of Egyptian civilization. The tomb of Horemheb, for example, the last pharaoh of the 18th Dynasty, is the first to be decorated with scenes from the *Book of Gates*, a funerary text that describes the journey of the sun god through the 12 gates of the 12 hours of darkness — a metaphor for the sun's perilous nighttime journey through the netherworld. It is from the tombs in the Valley of the Kings that we have learned much about the last great age of ancient Egyptian civilization.

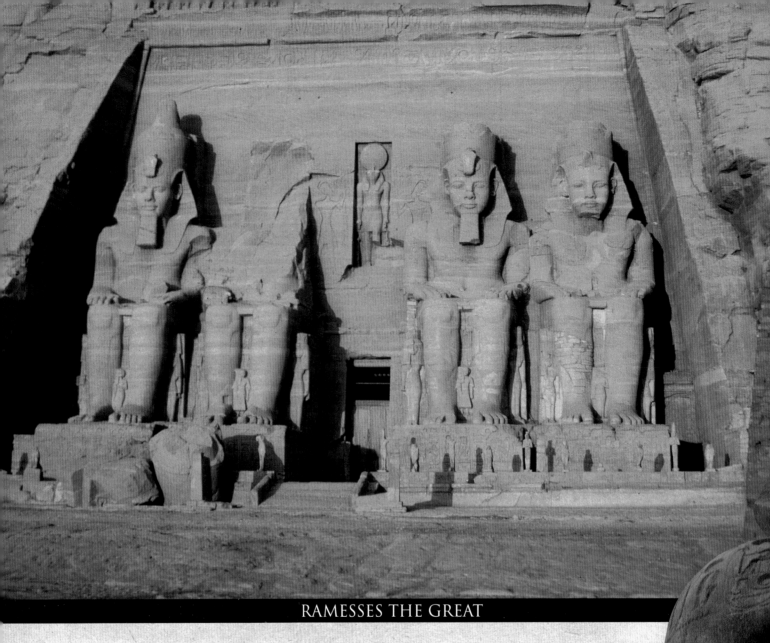

RAMESSES THE GREAT

If ever a ruler made his mark, it was Ramesses II, whose long and prosperous reign afforded him ample time to build his legacy of stone. So overwhelming are Ramesses' monuments to himself that they have tended to obscure those of other pharaohs, especially since many of them obliterated evidence of earlier monarchs. His most extreme act of self-aggrandization was likely his "great temple" at Abu Simbel (above), whose façade boasted four colossal seated statues of the pharaoh. The temple itself is far inferior to the one he built at Abydos earlier in his reign. However, it is so aligned that twice each year, once in February and once in October, the rising sun illuminates the statues of the gods within. To the ordinary Egyptian of his day, this ubiquitous and monumental pharaoh must have seemed great indeed.

(Left) The colossus of Luxor shows the divine aspect of Ramesses II. (Top) Wall paintings celebrate Ramesses' subjugation of Egypt's traditional vassals: Nubia, Syria, and Libya. The pharaoh was an active participant in battles like the one represented above, against the Nubians.

serious it may well have killed him. In the words of Bob Brier, author of *Egyptian Mummies*, "We can be sure that Ramesses' last days were spent in agony." The X-rays showed bundles in the abdominal cavity, wads of linen placed there to prevent the abdomen from caving in. And his heart appears to have been removed, then reattached, undoubtedly by gold threads, although it is on the wrong side of his chest cavity. But how much more could have been learned if the French team had been permitted to perform an autopsy. (A primitive endoscope was apparently used to look inside his body, but no tissue samples were taken.)

Ironically, a recently developed technology could have told the French even more about Ramesses the Great — the CAT scan, or CT scan. (CAT stands for Computed Axial Tomography.) This technique, a major advance over the conventional radiology practiced in Paris, makes a series of X-ray slices through the subject along different axes. When assembled by a computer program developed for the purpose, these multiple slices yield a detailed two-dimensional image far superior to a conventional X-ray. In 1976 the technology was in its infancy but rapidly gaining acceptance. The French missed a golden opportunity. Instead, history's first documented CAT scan of ancient Egyptian remains was performed in Toronto.

Today the refurbished mummy of Ramesses II lies in a climate-controlled display case in the Cairo Museum.

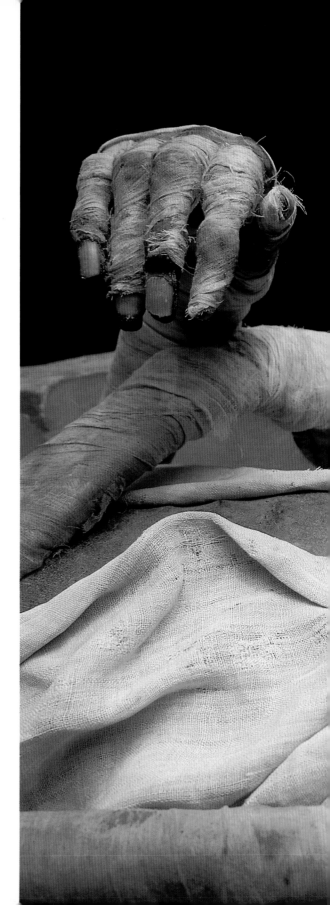

114

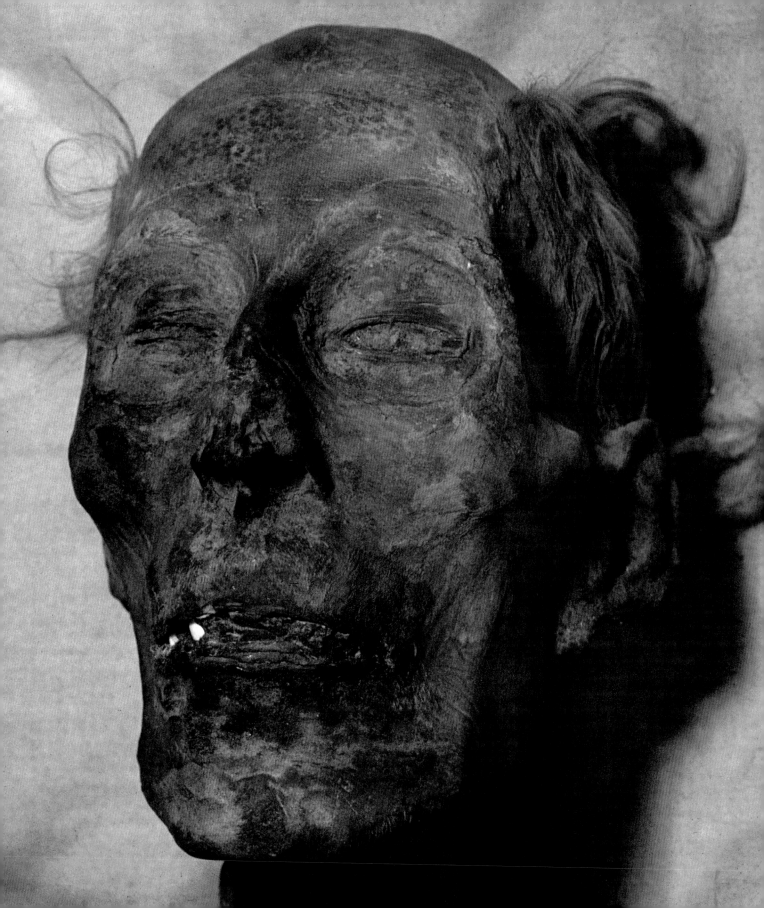

IN THE SUMMER OF 1975, HALF A YEAR BEFORE RAMESSES II BEGAN HIS ELABORATE REHABILITATION IN Paris, Toronto General Hospital acquired the city's first CAT scanner, an occasion that gave Gerald Hart and John Scott a bright idea: Why not test out this new technology on Nakht's brain? Hart remembers the ensuing episode with a mixture of disappointment and amusement. The technology turned out to be too rudimentary for tissue in which no fluid was present. Thus this pioneering attempt had to be judged a failure, except that it bequeathed Hart a classic mummy joke for future telling. When he had arrived with Nakht's brain at Toronto General, he informed the radiology receptionist, "I'm here for the CAT scan on my mummy." Moments later the following announcement went out over the department's intercom: "Have we done the scan on Dr. Hart's mother yet?"

By the fall of 1976, when Toronto's Hospital for Sick Children acquired its first CAT scan machine, the technology had advanced enough to make a second look at Nakht's gray matter seem worthwhile. At Hart's suggestion, Peter Lewin borrowed Nakht's brain from the Academy of Medicine museum, cleverly timing its withdrawal to coincide with the new machine's calibration. Thus, Nakht wouldn't be taking time from any living patients.

Despite the ravages of age and decay, the face of Ramesses the Great still hints at the powerful personality that dominated an empire.

The CAT scan of Nakht's brain lasted only a few minutes. In the words of a paper subsequently published by Lewin and his colleague Derek Harwood-Nash, director of neuroradiology at the Hospital for Sick Children who conducted the scan, "Computed tomographic images or brain slices 8 mm thick were obtained in the axial and coronal planes through both cerebral hemispheres lying side by side." The resulting images revealed the interior of the brain, including several white spots that probably represented areas of post-mortem calcification. In other words, Nakht's brain was perfectly normal. However much the young man may have suffered before his demise, it wasn't due to any brain disease.

Far more important, this pioneering mummy CAT scan proved that it was possible to "dissect" ancient tissue without using a scalpel. If such a dissection could be performed on an ancient brain, it could potentially be performed on an ancient body, even one that was wrapped in linen and sealed within an elaborately decorated body coffin. As Lewin realized, however, CAT technology was still in its early days, and the two-dimensional images of Nakht's brain left much to be desired. But surely the art of computer imaging would soon make it possible to convert two-dimensional slices into three-dimensional images of the insides of an ancient mummy. He was convinced that the CAT scan of Nakht's brain pointed the way to the first completely noninvasive analysis of ancient remains, the first virtual autopsy.

A view of the ancient workers' village
of Deir el Medina suggests what
Nakht's village must have been like.
(Above) A contemporary Egyptian boy
stands in front of a structure fashioned
from mud brick and limestone chips.

A CONVERSATION WITH NAKHT

What was Nakht's life like? Was it typical of the working class of his day? Here, as so often in Egyptology, we enter the realm of informed speculation. But thanks to the excellent analysis done on Nakht's remains, our speculation is based on some solid evidence. When these gleanings of mummy science are combined with the knowledge of more traditional Egyptology, an individual human being begins to emerge into the foreground.

Nakht is especially interesting to the student of ancient Egyptian social history because of his lowly status. Compared to the numerous records of pharaohs and high priests, we have relatively little information about working-class people. Palaces, tombs, and temples have survived; generally speaking, the mud-brick houses of workers have not. Only a handful of worker's villages have been discovered and excavated, and these tend to come from times much earlier than when Nakht lived. The best known of the villages that belong to Nakht's time is Deir el Medina, which housed the workers who built the tombs in the Valley of the Kings.

Nakht's home was a small village on the west bank of the Nile, close to Sethnakhte's temple, of which only a few stones survive. Of Nakht's village nothing at all remains. For any real sense of Nakht's world, we must walk the narrow streets of Deir el Medina, where single-story mud-brick houses were crowded side by side. In my mind's eye I can see an early morning scene: Nakht trails reluctantly behind his father — undoubtedly a weaver, who passed his craft on to his son — as they head off to work. Their fellow workers trudge quietly along the same streets to the village's single gate and thence to the fields and workshops of the nearby funerary temple of King Sethnakhte, the first pharaoh of the 20th Dynasty (1200-1085 B.C.E.).

We know from the inscription of Nakht's surprisingly fine coffin that he worked for Sethnakhte's memorial foundation, likely established soon after his death — he reigned a curt two years — by his son Ramesses III. Nakht and his fellow artisans labored in storehouses, plantations, and workshops to maintain Sethnakhte's temple and provide offerings that would assure his immortality. Most of the textiles from Nakht's workshop were either used to clothe the temple employees or sold to generate income.

In all likelihood, Ramesses III was the only pharaoh Nakht knew or could imagine, but I doubt he ever laid eyes upon his king. Even this late in Egyptian history, the pharaoh was like a god, whose existence was more mythic than real. By this time, the pharaoh probably visited Thebes only once a year for the Festival of Opet and one last time to be

buried; his court and his power were concentrated in the delta well to the north. But Nakht's world stretched only as far as the nearby banks of the Nile.

We can begin to fill in the details of that world by looking at literary sources, one of the best of which is a Middle Kingdom work known as *The Satire of the Trades*. This wonderful book takes the form of a humble man giving advice to his son, who is not applying himself to his studies. (In ancient Egypt a son generally followed his father's profession.) To persuade the student to stick to his studies, the father paints a contemptuous portrait of the more lowly, illiterate professions, or trades, to which he will sink if he fails his examinations. Here, for example, is his description of the Reed Mat Maker:

(Above) A tomb model shows a traditional weaver squatting before a horizontal loom. (Opposite) The same posture is employed by a modern weaver working on a similar loom.

> *The reed mat maker is in the weaving room;*
> *He is worse off than a woman.*
> *He squats with his knees against his belly,*
> *And he can't breathe air.*
> *If he wastes a day, not weaving,*
> *He is beaten with fifty strokes;*
> *He has to give his doorkeeper his lunch*
> *So he will let him out into the daylight.*

This is the closest the *Satire* comes to describing Nakht's profession, weaver of linen. During the Middle Kingdom (1991-1786 B.C.E.), linen weaving was performed almost exclusively by women because it was considered too lowly an activity for men, but with the introduction of the vertical loom during the early New Kingdom, men began to take up the trade. By Nakht's time, commercial weaving had become a predominantly male occupation, practiced in communal workshops, although women undoubtedly continued to weave at home.

Nakht and his fellow weavers presumably worked in a covered workshop — perhaps a roofed area inside a walled compound — squatting for long hours at their looms. Nearby sat more exalted workers: the scribal accountants, who kept a record of every item of raw material and every finished piece, and the doorkeepers, who acted as security guards. Support for such a picture comes from examining Nakht's skeleton. Like the great majority of ancient Egyptians, his "squatting facets," located on the tibia and talus bones, are highly developed — proof that he spent much of his waking life in a squatting position.

Since Nakht was only 15 when he died, it seems safe to assume he lived with his parents and brothers and sisters. (Egyptian families tended to be big then, as they do now.) When I try to picture him, I see him lounging on the roof of his family's tiny mud-brick house at the end of a hot and tiring working day. The sun has just set and, as it always does in a hot arid climate, the air already feels cool, even though the daytime temperature may have reached well over 100 degrees Fahrenheit (38 degrees Celsius). (In Nakht's time, the weather around Thebes was drier than it is today. The big lake created by the building of the Aswan dams has made the climate more humid and much less pleasant.)

As Nakht dozes, he can hear his young brothers and sisters playing in the house below while his mother prepares the evening meal. When she calls, he reluctantly climbs down the short steep steps and enters the house through the front door, stepping down into the main room, long and narrow like the house itself. In niches cut into the whitewashed walls repose images of local gods, far more important to Nakht's family than the state god who lives in the huge temple across the river in eastern Thebes. In addition to the main room, there are cell-like bedrooms and an open-air kitchen off the back of the house. (His father and mother likely sleep in the cool cellar below the main room.) The living room is shadowy and full of smoke from a guttering oil lamp that casts a feeble yellow light. Nakht begins to cough as soon as he enters, a deep, hacking cough that wracks his emaciated frame. When the coughing finally subsides, he takes his place, sitting cross-legged on a rush mat on the hard-packed mud floor.

Nakht's dinner is less than enough to keep body and soul together. These last few years the Nile has not flooded to its accustomed height, and many fields have been left dry and unplanted. Reduced harvests mean that many Egyptians — the poorest especially — have gone hungry. As Nakht coughs again, spitting up the meager fermented gruel the Egyptians called beer, his mother and father look at him with worry. If he cannot keep down his food, he will never get well. Their fears are well founded.

As Nakht's condition worsens, perhaps his mother climbs the hill near the village to visit the shrine of the goddess Hathor, a very positive deity responsible for beauty, love, sex, music, and the delights of intoxication, and who also cures sick children. Despite her prayers, however, Nakht's condition deteriorates as the weeks pass.

The poor weaver's last days on earth are miserable. His lungs burn and the pain in his stomach often causes him to double over in agony. He coughs constantly and can't seem to catch his breath. For some time he has been running a high fever and has been too feeble to work. One moment his body is on fire, the next it is trembling with chills. Near the end he slips in and out of a coma and gasps for air with rapid moaning breaths. Finally, his troubled breathing stops for good.

How could Nakht's family afford to bury him in a wooden coffin, which would have cost the equivalent of a month's wages? Perhaps a coffin was one of the perks of employment in a temple workshop. Or maybe one of Nakht's uncles was a coffin maker. As Nakht's autopsy showed, he was not embalmed, a process far too expensive for someone so poor. As for the linen bandages that wrapped his body, they were likely odd cuttings unwanted by more respectable customers. Perhaps he had helped weave some of them himself.

—*Rosalie David*

(Above) Villages in Egypt haven't changed much since ancient times, as this contemporary village scene of flat-roofed dwellings and narrow streets demonstrates. Modern Egyptian houses look remarkably like this soul house (right), which would have been placed at the entrance to a shaft-tomb belonging to a poorer person as late as the Middle Kingdom.

123

CHAPTER FOUR

A PAINFUL DEATH

S INCE 1910, THE BEAUTIFUL 22ND-DYNASTY BODY COFFIN OF A WOMAN NAMED DJEDMAATESANKH had ranked among the prized possessions of Toronto's Royal Ontario Museum. The gold leaf on the coffin's beautifully rendered face and the care with which the whole cartonnage case had been decorated signified that the coffin had been prepared for a person of some wealth and social standing. The style and choice of subject matter suggested a date very close to 850 B.C.E., far more precise than could be obtained through radiocarbon dating.

As was customary on coffins of this type and time, the name and title of the person it holds appear in hieroglyphs written above a painted figure of the deceased. Here Djedmaatesankh is shown approaching Osiris for judgment, led by Horus and followed by Thoth. Maat was the Egyptian goddess of truth, justice, and cosmic order. Literally translated, Djedmaatesankh's name means "The Goddess of Truth Has Said That She Will Live," and her honorific reads "chantress at the temple of Amun." The hieroglyphs also give the name of her mother, Shedtaope, and of her husband, Paankhntof, "doorkeeper at the temple of Amun," the great shrine of Amun-Re at Karnak in eastern Thebes, across the river from the mortuary temples and burial sites.

Egyptian given names often incorporated the names of gods. Djedmaatesankh's includes the name of the goddess of truth, Maat, here seen as she was portrayed in the tomb of Ramesses I.

Under the scrutiny of an Egyptologist, the coffin and its simple inscriptions become amazingly suggestive. For example, it was standard practice for the name of the deceased's mother to appear — she had brought Djed into this world and would help take her into the next — but not for the name of the husband. Paan's presence presumably means he helped pay for the cost of mummification and burial. Was this a sign of affection or simply a statement of status? If he paid for everything — the embalming, the expensive coffin, the funeral — it likely cost him the equivalent of a year's salary. That Djed and her husband could afford such fancy funerary accoutrements makes it likely they belonged to the upper middle class.

And what of the titles "chantress" and "doorkeeper"? Are they to be taken literally? Did Djed

THE ART OF DJED'S COFFIN

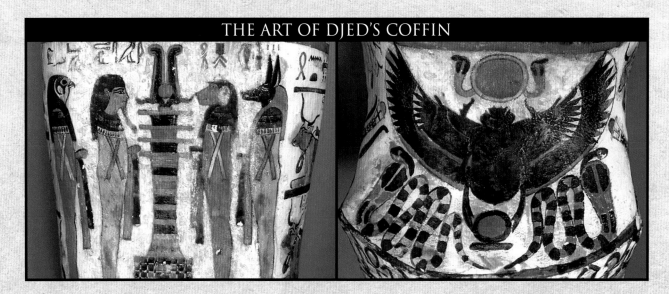

The cartonnage coffin of Djedmaatesankh shows the care with which the Egyptians of the 22nd Dynasty buried those who could afford the full funeral treatment. Read from bottom to top, Djed's coffin (opposite) presents a neat anthology of standard funerary iconography of the period. The winged scarab (shown in detail above right) represents the sun god in his morning form, symbolic of resurrection. At the next level, the four sons of Horus flank a pillar that represents the god Osiris (shown in detail above left). Note that the pillar is topped by a crown consisting of the sun disk flanked by ram's horns, standard headgear for Osiris. The next level portrays the portable boat shrine of Sokar, a god of death from the northern city of Memphis. Then comes the Osiris fetish, a basket (atop a pillar) that represents the basket containing Osiris's dismembered head. And finally comes the standard scene showing the deceased being led before Osiris.

The four sons of Horus find their female counterparts in the four vulture-winged goddesses, Isis, Nepthys, Neith, and Selket (below). All four are visible flanking the scenes on the front of Djed's coffin (opposite and right).

spend her days singing songs in praise of Amun while her husband Paan idled away long hours guarding the temple door? As with almost every aspect of the ancient Egyptian world, we can't be sure, but the titles certainly came along with some responsibilities. They indicate that Djed and Paan were members of the lay priesthood. (The temples at Karnak and Luxor were the main economic engines of the Theban economy and would have employed thousands of lay priests.)

One month in every three, Djed and her husband would leave their regular lives, perhaps as well-off owners of an estate on the banks of the Nile, to undertake their religious duties. Following rituals of purification that included washing the body and shaving the head, they would have joined the legions of lay priests and priestesses whose job it was to maintain the temple and attend to the care and feeding of the deity. Each day the god was presented with food offerings, later consumed by the priests (one of the perks of temple duty). Djed may well have sung in praise of Amun, or played a primitive instrument — *chantress* is probably a generic word for musician — and Paan likely wielded a nasty-looking club as he stood guard at the temple door, bowing in respect as the high priests entered.

Beyond these educated guesses, however, the lives of Djedmaatesankh and Paankhntof become more difficult to parse. Were they happy? Were they healthy? Did they have children? A lively social life? On these subjects the coffin is silent. From other sources, however, we know that the 22nd Dynasty (945-730 B.C.E.) in the Third Intermediate Period was a time of turmoil in Egypt. The descendants of Libyan mercenaries had usurped the royal line of Egyptian kings and wielded power from their capital, Bubastis, in the delta to the north. These pharaohs of foreign extraction had adopted the local religious customs, but they seldom if ever came to Thebes and were not buried in the Valley of the Kings. Undoubtedly, royal offerings to Amun-Re had grown scarce, and Thebes, the ancient political and religious capital, was not as wealthy as it had once been.

But for all the accumulated wisdom of a century and a half of Egyptology, the woman inside the beautiful coffin remained an alluring enigma. In order to unwrap her mystery, the sealed coffin would have to be dismantled, irrevocably damaging a priceless piece of ancient art. That was quite clearly out of the question — unless Djedmaatesankh could somehow be examined without her coffin being harmed.

128

What did ancient Egyptian music sound like? From the many surviving images of musical instruments and of music being played, we can make some reasonable guesses. By the time of the New Kingdom, an Egyptian orchestra could comprise a remarkable number of music makers. Stringed instruments included the harp, quite possibly Egyptian in origin (seen opposite at right, inset below, and at far right), as well as the lute and the lyre. In addition to the flute, another instrument that may have been invented in Egypt, a surprising number of wind instruments were played: the clarinet, double oboe, and trumpet or bugle. Percussion instruments seem to have been the most common of all, including tambourines, various drums, and the distinctive Egyptian rattle called the *sistrum*. All of these, in varying combinations and settings, were almost always accompanied by the human voice and often provided occasion for dancing, either sacred or profane. Since musical notation did not exist, however, the tunes the Egyptians played and sang are lost to eternity.

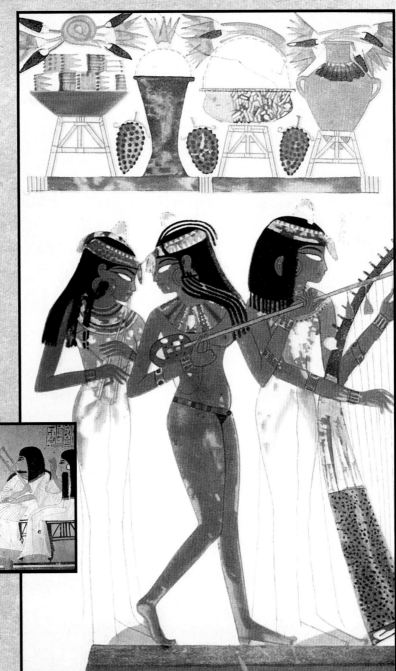

129

EVER SINCE THE 1976 CAT SCAN OF NAKHT'S BRAIN, PETER LEWIN OF TORONTO'S HOSPITAL FOR SICK Children had been thinking about the potential for this rapidly evolving technology. About a year later, he approached Nicholas Millet, curator of Egyptology at the Royal Ontario Museum, with the idea of performing a whole-mummy CAT scan. Until now, the ROM curator had resisted any further medical analysis of the mummies in his keeping, but he'd been impressed by Lewin's work on Nakht, and he was open to the idea. When the doctor convinced him that Djed's case would not be touched and the mummy inside in no way damaged, Millet readily agreed. He was as curious as anyone to learn more about the person inside the coffin.

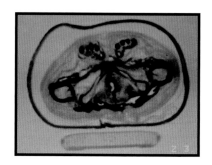

(Above) A single X-ray slice from Djed's first CAT scan shows several recognizable features, including her pelvis, on lower left, and her hands, at top. (Opposite) Djed's untouched coffin enters the scanner.

On the afternoon of November 9, 1977, an ambulance made the brief trip from the loading dock at the Royal Ontario Museum to the receiving dock at the Hospital for Sick Children. There Djed's coffin was unloaded with "*utmost* care," placed on a gurney, and trundled to the Radiology Department. Once again, Lewin's colleague at the Hospital for Sick Children, Derek Harwood-Nash, by now an enthusiastic adherent of mummy science, presided. Two hours later, Djed made the return trip to the Royal Ontario Museum. Except for that day's visitors to the ROM's Egyptian galleries, few knew that Djed had ever left her display case.

Here is Lewin's account of the CAT scan results: "Superb detail was obtained of the mummy within the cartonnage. For example, tomographic sections of the head showed prosthetic artificial eyes set in the eye sockets. The cranial cavity was stuffed with linen wadding and bandages, the brain having been removed through the right nostril and cribiform plate of the skull, which was fractured. Sections through the pelvis showed normal hip joints, and within the pelvic cavity, remains of the uterus could be observed. Various religious artifacts were enclosed in the mummy wrapping, as was a gold plate on the left flank of the abdomen." (Such plates were commonly used to cover the evisceration incision.) A CAT scan can determine the type of metal from the angle at which it refracts the X-rays.

As far as can be ascertained, Djedmaatesankh was the first Egyptian mummy — the first ancient human being — to undergo a whole-body CAT scan. More important, the experience proved the potential of computerized tomography, then still in its early stages. As with Nakht's brain, the images of Djed were two-dimensional. But by making carefully aimed X-ray slices through a subject, the scanner could isolate and examine places of particular interest and create pictures of sufficient detail that objects in the mummy's wrappings could be identified. As well as the gold plate, the scan revealed opaque plates covering Djed's eyes and a bird amulet on her breast.

As DJED BECAME A LITTLE LESS ENIGMATIC, THE WIDER WORLD OF MUMMY SCIENCE WAS GROWING fast. By 1979, Aidan Cockburn's pioneering autopsy work had spawned investigations by Egyptologists, anthropologists, physicians, and histologists around the globe. Studies continued on South American mummies, on mummies in the Canary Islands, and on the remarkably preserved bodies of long-deceased woolly mammoths that had recently emerged from the Siberian icecap. By its nature, paleopathology is a many-faceted endeavor, requiring expertise in fields as varied as ancient funerary practices and molecular biology. And nowhere was the multidisciplinary approach practiced with more vigor than at the University of Manchester, where the Manchester Mummy Project continued to gather momentum.

Since the 1975 autopsy of Mummy 1770, Rosalie David and her colleagues had not been idle. Two teaching films had grown out of the event, as well as two books, one a popular account of the autopsy and its findings, the other a more scholarly tome. As their work became more widely known, the Manchester team made connections with other researchers in the field. Soon it became obvious that the time was ripe for an event that would bring together the far-flung students of life and death in the ancient Near East. The resulting symposium, "Science in Egyptology," held in Manchester in the summer of 1979, involved more than a hundred participants who read papers on subjects ranging from "Experimental Mummification of Rats" to "Possibilities, Limitations and Prospects of Computed Tomography as a Non-invasive Method of Mummy Studies." By the end of the conference, the way ahead for Manchester seemed clear: It would pioneer the use of medical endoscopes on mummies.

Medical endoscopy may well be as old as the oldest of the mummies that Rosalie has studied. A 12th-Dynasty (1991-1786 B.C.E.) statuette formerly in the Mariemont Museum in Belgium depicts a man sitting behind a kneeling woman, his hands resting firmly on her bare buttocks. He is apparently looking at or into her anus. While this could be a piece of ancient pornography, more likely it represents a doctor performing an anuscopy. Ancient Egyptian medicine was highly specialized. Some Egyptologists believe that the person described in the Ebers medical papyrus as the "Shepherd of the anus" may well have been an intestinal specialist. (Or he may merely have been the palace retainer responsible for administering the royal enemas.) Herodotus later commented that the Egyptians seemed to be obsessed with the movements of their bowels.

By 1980, medical endoscopes had advanced light years beyond their recent predecessors, which consisted of hollow rigid tubes with electric lights on the probing end. When such an instrument was inserted into a bodily orifice it caused great discomfort to the patient — not least because of the heat from the tiny lightbulb. But by the time the Mummy Project began looking for a suitable endoscope, the options included incredibly slender long flexible fiberscopes, which take advantage of the applied science of fiberoptics. In a fiberscope, a bundle of tiny transparent fibers transports light in both directions — from a powerful light source to the interior of the patient and from the object being examined back to the viewer's eye. The slender fibers permit the light to follow a curved path without distorting the image.

As her colleague Dr. Edmund Tapp comments, "Rosalie has a knack for getting people to volunteer their time." Since co-directing the 1975 autopsy of Mummy 1770, Tapp had spent many of

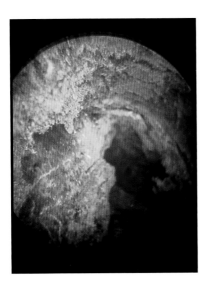 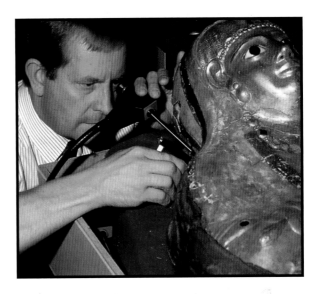

Ken Wildsmith (right) peers into an endoscope inserted inside the body cavity of Mummy 1776 from the Manchester Museum collection. The quality of the image Wildsmith has to work with (left) will depend on the space available for him to maneuver the scope. Tiny forceps attached to the scope's end permit the taking of tissue samples.

his spare hours studying mummy tissue. Now he made endoscopy his personal project. This meant borrowing a suitable instrument, since buying one — at a price of about five thousand pounds — was out of the question. Understandably, however, his colleagues in the Gastroenterology Department at the Preston Infirmary were reluctant. They needed their endoscope for live patients.

Enter Ken Wildsmith, a Manchester salesman with Keymed Limited, a British manufacturer of medical and industrial instruments. (Fiberscopes are used for many delicate industrial applications, including looking for faults inside internal combustion engines.) One day the office received a call from an Egyptologist at the Manchester Museum, inquiring about endoscopes, and Wildsmith went off to sell one to the museum. By the end of his interview with Rosalie David, he'd offered to join her team and find it an endoscope. Then he set about persuading his company that lending Rosalie an instrument would be good publicity. He's been a part of the Mummy Project ever since.

As Wildsmith says now, a more unlikely Egyptologist would be hard to find. He hadn't the slightest interest in Egypt, ancient or modern. Despite living in Manchester, he'd completely missed all the media hoopla when Mummy 1770 had been autopsied. But he loved a technical challenge, immediately saw that current medical endoscopes probably wouldn't work on mummies, and began the task of adapting an existing one to suit this special purpose.

Medical endoscopes don't require much light, because they are looking at living tissue, which is shiny and highly reflective. Ken realized that a mummy endoscopy would be more like sending an industrial scope into the "dark dirty non-reflective" innards of an engine where, as the saying goes, "you're looking for black cats in black coal cellars." In the end, he adapted an instrument designed for examining the inaccessible empty space between the walls of traditionally built English houses. For taking tissue samples, he attached a set of biopsy forceps to the scope's end with electrical duct tape.

I N CONTRAST TO THE VERY PUBLIC AUTOPSY OF MUMMY 1770, THE PIONEERING ENDOSCOPY IN THE annals of Egyptology was a very private affair, held in a small nondescript room at the Manchester Museum. Only four people were present: Rosalie David, Edmund Tapp, Ken Wildsmith, and a woman named Asru.

The mummy of Asru, acquired in 1825, had arrived unwrapped and without bandages but with two inscribed body coffins, one fitting neatly within the other. Between her legs a package was visible, presumably containing some or all of her viscera. Like the ROM's Djedmaatesankh, she had lived in Thebes and been honored with the title "chantress of Amun," but she had probably lived much later than Djed, during the Third Intermediate Period, Rosalie guessed, about 700 B.C.E., which would place her in the 25th Dynasty.

In the early 1970s, as the Mummy Project was getting underway, Asru's innards had provided samples for some of the team's earliest examinations of mummy tissue. Under the microscope, the tissue in the package, which proved to be her intestines, showed evidence of strongyles, parasitic worms with a complex life cycle, which infest both the intestines and the lungs.

Rosalie hoped that endoscopy would add to the picture of Asru's medical condition. Regardless, the experiment would determine how effective the technique would be at probing the dark "coal cellar" within an ancient Egyptian body. The three learned as they went. With Dr. Tapp directing and Ken Wildsmith "driving" the probe, they explored all three of Asru's main body cavities — chest, abdomen, and skull — recovering tissue samples from each one. Trickiest was the skull, which had to be entered through one of the eye sockets. The obvious route via the nose septum, pierced by the embalmers to remove her brain, was blocked because her nose had collapsed.

It turned out that Asru had been a very sick lady. In addition to the strongyles infection previously discovered, she had a hydatid cyst in her lungs. (Such cysts are caused by a parasitic worm found in dog feces.) Asru, like all those who lived before human beings learned how diseases are spread, didn't know to wash her hands before eating. During life, Asru would have coughed and wheezed from shortness of breath, often suffered from diarrhea accompanied by blood in her stool, and lived with a chronic stomach ache. Yet it seems that she lived to a ripe old age. Her aorta and several important arteries showed calcification typical of advanced years, and the middle finger of her left hand had been deformed by osteoarthritis. Asru also exhibited a skull defect suggestive of a metastatic tumor. She may have had bone cancer.

The 1980 examinations of Asru and other Manchester mummies proved the viability of endoscopy as a technique in mummy science, and over the next few years, Tapp and Wildsmith became increasingly adept at this delicate and difficult work. Wildsmith has taken all the Mummy Project's endoscopic

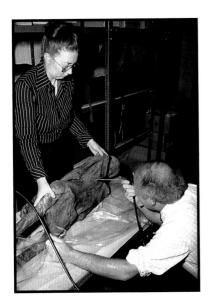

(Above) Rosalie David assists with the endoscopy of Asru. (Right) The mummy of the ancient chantress.

photographs, making him the undoubted world-record holder in this arcane area. All the while, he kept tinkering with the technology, eventually settling on the perfect instrument: a portable flexible industrial fiberscope designed for use in servicing jet engines. It is a hand-held unit with a small video screen and rechargeable battery belt, which can be taken almost anywhere — including on field trips to Egypt. (The Royal Air Force uses the same scope for front-line inspection of its Tornado and Jaguar fighter aircraft.)

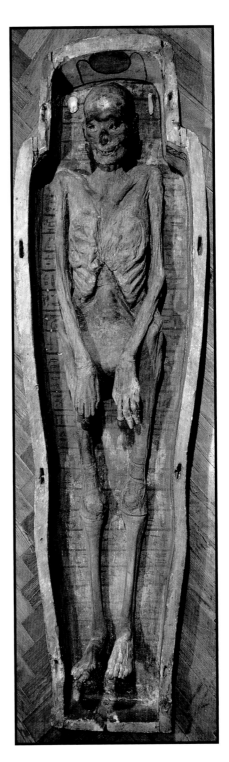

The Manchester Mummy Project went on to endoscope many more mummies, in whole or in part, proving beyond any doubt the usefulness of this technology to mummy science. On one of these the Manchester group also employed a full-body CAT scan, possibly the first time both an endoscope and computed tomography had been used on the same ancient subject. Other researchers also experimented with CAT scans, ranging from Boston's Museum of Fine Arts to the famed British Museum in London. But not until 1994 would the full potential of the technology be decisively demonstrated.

Before the second CAT scan of Djedmaatesankh, Peter Lewin tested the rapidly improving technology on a mummified cat.

SINCE THE PIONEERING WHOLE-MUMMY CAT SCAN OF DJED IN 1977, the Toronto researchers had continued to experiment with the technology. In 1986, Peter Lewin and two colleagues produced 3-D reconstructions of several mummified heads dating from the Greco-Roman Period (332 B.C.E.-ca. 600 C.E.). A month later, they successfully scanned a mummified cat. But not until the early 1990s had the technology advanced to the point where a fully three-dimensional image of an intact mummy inside its coffin and wrappings could theoretically be conjured from the computer hieroglyphs of CAT-scan data. The time was ripe for a second scan of Djedmaatesankh.

Peter Lewin likes to joke that the 1994 CAT scan of Djedmaatesankh must have been the first time a patient both arrived at and left from the hospital in a hearse. (The hearse was lent to him by one of his patients.) Outwardly, Djed's time away from the Royal Ontario Museum passed much as it had in 1977. This time, however, she spent four full hours inside the CAT machine, far longer than a live patient could safely endure.

Under the skilled direction of Hospital for Sick Children medical radiation technologist Stephanie Holowka, Djed received a CAT scan like no mummy before her. In some ways, scanning a mummy is easier than scanning a live person: The subject doesn't move and can't suffer from a radiation overdose. But when it comes to producing a clear picture, a mummy presents a much greater challenge.

In essence, a CAT scanner is an X-ray machine that looks at its subject from every direction — all 360 degrees — making a series of images in the form of slender slices, or cross-sections, through the body. Each of these cross-sections cuts right through the subject being scanned, revealing every level – from its outermost skin to its innermost organs. Once the scan is complete, a computer program stacks the cross-sections together — Holowka compares them to slices of bread being stacked back into a loaf — creating a detailed image of the targeted area. Thanks to recent advances in computer software, Stephanie was able to manipulate the CAT scanner's two-dimensional slices into three-dimensional images.

The problem with scanning a mummy is one of relative densities. The scanner differentiates between skin, bone, and tissue by comparing its density to that of water. The denser the material, the lighter it appears on the scan. Living bone is very dense and looks almost white. Skin or fat is

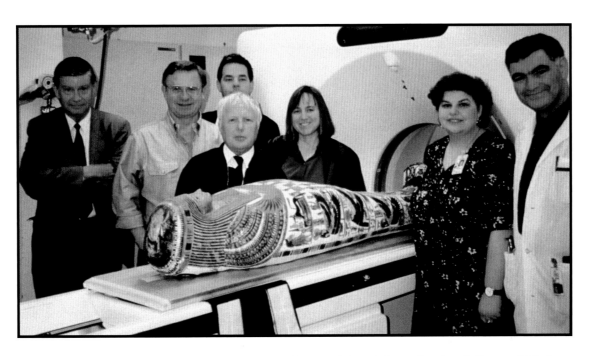

Most of the team involved in the 1994 scan of Djed: (left to right) Nicholas Millet, Derek Harwood-Nash, Alan Hollett, David McEachnie (back row), Marianne Webb, Stephanie Holowka, and Peter Lewin.

less dense and comes out in shades of gray. Liquids such as blood are the least dense of all and show up on the scan as black. But in a mummy the bone has softened and become less dense, the soft tissues have hardened and become denser, and water has disappeared. Before being put through the computer reconstruction program, the CAT scan of Djed would show up mostly as shades of gray.

During the actual scan, Holowka made many more slices through Djed than she would have made through a living patient — a total of three hundred. These varied in thickness, from 1.5 mm for details of the skull, such as the ears, to 3 mm for the skull itself, and 5 mm for the rest of the body. Even before the information from these multiple cross-sections was fed into the computer's reconstruction program, they delivered a great deal of information, including the fact that the former chantress of Amun had some sort of cyst in her jaw.

Once the scan was complete and Djedmaatesankh had safely made the return trip by hearse to the Royal Ontario Museum, it was time for Holowka to begin her real work: reconstructing an ancient body from a mass of digital data. She accomplished this feat by laboriously editing each and every slice of Djed for both structure and density. (Most reconstruction programs only allow editing for density.) Because of the mummy's narrow range of densities, Stephanie's editing took much longer than normal. For example, a living head usually takes her fifteen to twenty minutes to reconstruct; Djed's head required two hours. In all, Holowka spent several hundred hours building up a detailed computer archive that represented Djed as she is today inside her beautiful body case.

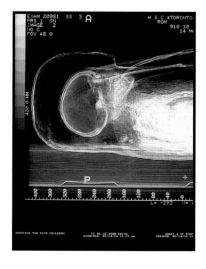

Having created the archive, Holowka could now use her specialized software to massage the three-dimensional images into sharper focus. Her most fascinating challenge was building an accurate picture of Djedmaatesankh's face as it had appeared in life. By examining the bones of her skull, Stephanie could get an inkling of what Djed looked like. "I could see that she had very fine features: high cheekbones and a well-defined chin," Stephanie recalls. "I realized she must have been a very pretty lady." Gradually, Djed was growing into someone she felt she knew.

But it took Holowka eight hours of editing skull slices one by one by one by one to build the flesh and skin surface up from the skull into a reasonable, though still far from perfect, facsimile of the original. Next, medical imaging specialist Mike Starr spent several hours refining what Stephanie had done. But she still wasn't satisfied. So Toronto police artist Betté Clark was called in to paint Djed's portrait from computer pictures of her skull — much as she would have done with photographs of a crime victim. Thus, the ancient art of life drawing and the modern art of computed axial tomography joined to create the living, and deceptively happy, face of Djedmaatesankh (opposite right).

Overall, the CAT scan painted a bleak picture compared to the idyllic image conveyed by Djed's colorful coffin. Her bones were poorly mineralized, perhaps as a result of malnutrition from chronic disease but more likely due to the effects of natron, and she had died childless — a great shame to a woman of her era. (The scans revealed that Djed's pelvis was intact. During childbirth the two pubic bones that form part of the pelvis separate as the infant emerges.)

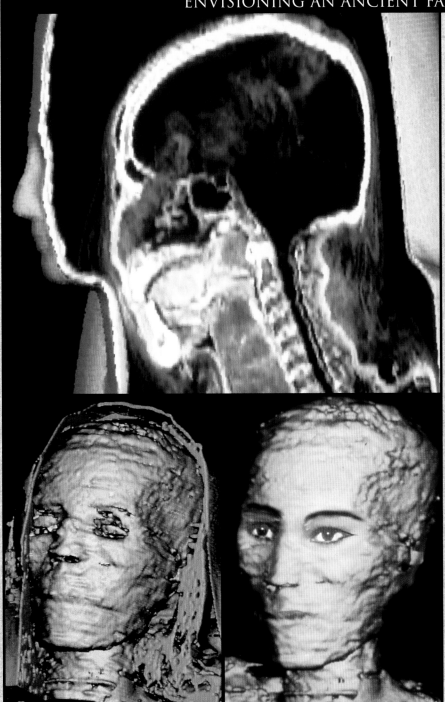

A full-body CAT scan of Djedmaatesankh's mummy made it possible to view the contents of the mummy case without ever opening it. Using a sophisticated computer program, scientists were able to electronically remove both the mummy case and the layers of linen wrapping surrounding the mummy to reveal clearer images of Djed's funerary jewelry (a gold vulture-shaped amulet and a stone heart scarab), her skin and bones, and finally, several carefully wrapped packages containing her embalmed internal organs.

To reconstruct Djed's skull, resins and linen wrappings were successively removed from the computer images of her head and face. An imaging specialist took the resulting scanned images and reshaped Djed's nose and mouth which had become misshapen from the tight linen bandages. This created an image of a beautiful woman — a face as compelling today as it must have been 3,000 years ago.

Sophisticated computer imaging allowed Stephanie Holowka to examine Djed's dental cyst in remarkable detail. (Left) The abscess appears as a black hole on the right side of this picture (the left side of Djed's jaw). It has grown so large that the bone tissue has distorted. (Below) A computerized reconstruction of Djed's skull employs a "translucency view" to isolate the abscess (in the black rectangle), starkly revealing its large size in relationship to her head.

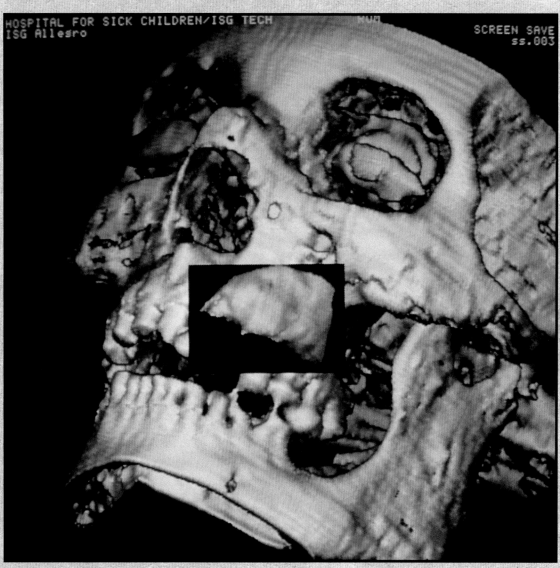

In three dimensions, Djed's dental cyst resolved into an enormous abscess that probably caused her death. The cyst, located within the bone of her upper left jaw, measured roughly 1 inch, or 2.54 cm, in diameter. In our age of antibiotics and sophisticated dentistry, few die of dental disease, but fatal dental infections must have been common in ancient Egypt. As the dental examinations of many mummies — including PUM-II — have shown, most adult Egyptians exhibit severe dental attrition: their teeth were worn down to the pulp because of the sand in their diet. (The sand was introduced both accidentally and deliberately. Ancient millers added sand to grain in order to grind it more finely.) And once the pulp is exposed, it easily becomes infected, giving rise to just the sort of septic cyst that led to Djed's death.

As her abscess grew, it would have become increasingly painful, begun to distort her face, and caused her breath to reek. According to dental scientist Tony Melcher, who helped analyze Djed's dental state, the exposed pulp would have caused Djed a "sharp acute pain, a most awful pain. Anything, even breathing in cold air, would hurt. Trying to eat would hurt enormously. Then the tooth would hurt of its own accord; it would ache." Days or perhaps weeks before she died, the cyst had burst, sending the infected pus into her bloodstream, putting a swift end to her misery. Djed's dental cyst vividly demonstrated that a virtual autopsy can sometimes reveal information that a literal one would have missed. Unless you were looking for an abscess, you would not dissect the skull.

Djed likely also suffered from at least one of the parasitic diseases that have been found in almost every mummy whose tissues have been studied. An endoscope could have probed Djed's tissues for further evidence of disease, but only by boring a series of tiny holes in her coffin. The CAT-scan approach means that her coffin remains intact and gleaming, a highlight of the Royal Ontario Museum's Egyptian gallery.

Outwardly, Djed may look the same, but for the people who know her best, the teachers in the museum's Education Department, a relationship has fundamentally changed. Every day during the school year, they shepherd scores of schoolchildren through the Egyptian gallery, giving them a glimpse into an ancient world. As teacher Gayle Gibson puts it, "Djemma had become our friend." Gayle has always called Djedmaatesankh "Djemma." "'Djed' sounds to harsh," she says.

The news of Djed's painful final days came as shock. "There were tears," Gayle admits, "when we discovered that Djed had lived through a long and agonizing final illness. We felt very bad that she had suffered so much."

Gayle Gibson probably knows as much as anyone about Djedmaatesankh. She can take you on a tour of her coffin as fascinating as any boat trip down the Nile, pointing out the tiny details that transform it from a lovely but essentially generic artifact into the work of individuals. She takes

BREAD AND BEER

The tomb painting above depicts the many stages of harvest, from mowing the grain with sickles, to transporting and gleaning the sheaths. Scribes are depicted measuring the grain and making a record of the harvest.

The two staples of the ancient Egyptian diet both came from grain: bread and beer. Attempts to follow the ancient beer recipe have yielded a barely palatable mildly fermented porridge made from barley or wheat, to which dates, honey, and spices might be added. The bread tastes better, but beware its hidden ingredient: sand. The finest Egyptian loaves came from the most finely ground flour, only obtainable through the addition of sand during the grinding process. Thus even most royal teeth show serious attrition. Egyptian bread was made from emmer-wheat and ground by rolling a round stone on a saddle quern (left). The loaves were often baked in conical molds and it is these, sliced lengthwise and laid out as an offering, that are often seen in tombs. (The association of bread and offering was so strong that the hieroglyph for the word *offering* takes the form of a loaf of bread on a slab.) Another form of funerary bread was baked with ear-shaped appendages meant to hear the prayers offered for the deceased (above right). Simple round loaves were the common bread of the common people. Wealthier folk could afford various pastries, sweetened with honey and studded with fruit.

great delight in pointing to the painted figure of Djed and noting that unlike the "doll faces" on most females' coffins, Djed's has a quite prominent jaw. Probably, she surmises, the artist knew Djed when she was alive and added this individual touch, making a generic figure into the beginnings of an individual portrait.

But knowing Djed during her final illness cannot have been pleasant, she admits. Her constant pain would have made her ill tempered and quite possibly abusive. Gayle points to one of the seven cows of Hathor, whose collective job is to make sure that the deceased has plenty of food in the afterlife. As was customary, each of the seven cows is named in hieroglyphs. The name above this particular cow is all wrong, however, she says. The hieroglyphs, which include a bull's penis, mean "bull, husband of cows." Such a mistake seems too obvious not to have been deliberate. Even an illiterate worker in the coffin shop knew a bull from a cow. Perhaps it was the coffin painter's private joke, she muses, or, just possibly, an act of derision for the foul-mouthed, foul-smelling person inside, a comment analogous to our expression, "the bull in the china shop."

This detail from the coffin of Djedmaatesankh shows the errant cow, in middle, whose name has been miswritten as "bull, husband of cows."

Since the CAT scan of Djedmaatesankh, Gayle Gibson has had to rewrite what she calls "the novel of Djed's life." Did her husband pay for the fancy coffin, she wonders, out of guilt? Since Djed hadn't given him any children, perhaps he'd grown fond of the family maid and fathered several offspring by her. But Gayle doesn't dwell on the pain and sadness of Djemma's last days. She prefers to imagine her as a much younger woman, living a good life in a lovely place.

"I like to think of her enjoying a beautiful sunset over the pink hills that loom in the distance, the river moving along so slowly and so beautifully. I can see the flags flying from the great pylons of the temple, announcing that the god is at home. I can hear the temples full of music, music played and sung by Djemma and her friends.

"In those days she had a loving husband and she must have been a beautiful woman. She lived in a beautiful place and her world was full of sunshine and color. She was financially secure and a person of status in her society. And she had the comfort of believing that her life would continue in the next world."

A CONVERSATION WITH DJED AND ASRU

I find it fascinating that these two women — so far removed from us in time and now residing on opposite sides of the Atlantic — have so much in common. By a remarkable coincidence, Asru could almost have known Djedmaatesankh. Both were attached to the temple of Amun at Karnak. Both bore the title "chantress of Amun," an honorific assigned to members of the lay priesthood who sang to the god during temple rituals. It is tempting to imagine their voices raised together in praise of Amun as each played on a tambourine or shook a ritual rattle called a *sistrum*, whose tinkling sound was believed to appease the god and chase away evil spirits.

That their lives actually overlapped, or even intersected, seems improbable. But given the inexactitude of ancient dating, the faint possibility exists that Djed and Asru shared the same space and time. Regardless, their bodies are now experiencing an afterlife far different from any they could have imagined.

The best date we have for Djed — 850 B.C.E. — is more than a hundred years earlier than the much less precise date we've assigned to Asru, who probably lived during the 25th Dynasty, which began around 780 B.C.E. Egyptian politics was very messy during this period. The 22nd Dynasty, when Djed lived, was followed by a confusion of overlapping dynasties.

When Djed was born, Egypt was ruled by an upstart dynasty of "foreigners," descendants of Libyan mercenaries who had arrived in Egypt as prisoners of war after their defeat at the hands of Ramesses III many years earlier, in roughly 1170 B.C.E. As this dynasty gradually collapsed, it gave way to a period of political upheaval when regional sub-dynasties competed for dominance as the central power grew increasingly weak. By the time Asru was born, centralized rule had been re-established by a dynasty of kings hailing from Egypt's southern province of

Nubia. Despite the political broils that characterized this era of flux, Djed's and Asru's worlds must have been quite similar. The magnificent temple at Karnak continued as the headquarters of the state religion, though the royal offerings that helped support its grandeur must have fallen off during the

(Opposite) A scene from Djed's coffin shows her being led to an enthroned Osiris by the falcon-headed god Horus. (Left) Two sistra. The sistrum was an Egyptian rattle used by temple musicians.

worst periods of unrest. One can only speculate to what degree the uneasy mood of the times affected these two women. But it is possible to outline the contours of their daily lives with a fair degree of accuracy.

The title "chantress" and the expensive manner of their burials mark both these women as privileged members of the upper middle class of one of Egypt's most important cities. Their temple duties likely constituted the most onerous aspects of their otherwise very comfortable lives, requiring them to

rise well before dawn so as to be in place in the temple's inner sanctum for the waking of Amun. Here is the morning hymn they would have sung on festival days as dawn's fingers first caressed the limestone hills of western Thebes.

> *The doors are opened at the Sanctuary,*
> *   the shrine is thrown open in the Mansion.*
> *Thebes is in festivity, Heliopolis in joy,*
> *   Karnak in rejoicing.*
> *Jubilation [fills] heaven and earth . . .*
> *Song is made for this noble god Amun-Re,*
> *Lord of the Thrones of the Two Lands,*
> *   [and] Amun, Lord of Luxor.*
> *His fragrance has encompassed the circuit*
> *   of the Great Green [Sea].*
> *Heaven and earth are full of his beauty,*
> *He has bathed them in gold with his rays . . .*

When they were not on temple duty, Djed and Asru probably lived in comfortable three-story townhouses with all sorts of amenities. They slept between linen sheets on low wooden beds with webbing where we would have a mattress and a headrest where we would use a soft pillow. Each house would have been equipped with a bathroom, always with a full pitcher of water at the ready for a "shower" or to flush the simple toilet (a squatting toilet much like those that used to be common in Europe). If there was a walled garden, the family gardener used it to cultivate fruit trees, vegetables, and flowers. (The Egyptians are the first people in recorded history to have cultivated flowers for pleasure.) Perhaps their walls were painted with scenes from mythology or with decorative motifs. Their floors were swept by housemaids, their food prepared by the family cook. If Asru had children, they would have been raised by a nurse. Depending on their status, they may have had thirty servants or more. If their husbands were important enough, they might even have owned a country villa with gardens and orchards and fresh country air.

Let us imagine Asru on the second day of the annual Feast of Opet, the greatest of the many festivals that punctuated the Theban year. This is the day that the portable barques bearing the images of Amun, Mut, and Khons make the ritual journey from Karnak to Luxor, leading up to a grand river trip accompanied by a flotilla of ships and a

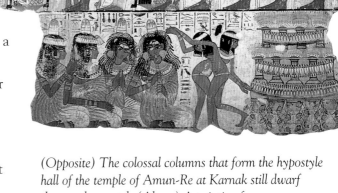

(Opposite) The colossal columns that form the hypostyle hall of the temple of Amun-Re at Karnak still dwarf the merely mortal. (Above) A painting from an 18th-Dynasty tomb at Thebes shows that the ancient Egyptians knew how to have a good time.

procession of dancers and musicians on shore. Since it is not Asru's turn at temple duty, she and her family can look forward to watching the parade and ending the day with a banquet at home.

Asru and her husband dress early in their finest pleated linen robes. She puts on her heavy black wig and spends a good hour manicuring her nails and applying her makeup with the help of her chambermaid. After breakfast, she and her husband lead their children along the streets of the city to the river, joining the crowds gathered at the temple quay to watch the gods arrive. The children are especially excited because they've been told that the pharaoh himself will accompany the temple procession. This is the one feast that the king always tries to attend.

As the great temple barge, burnished in gold foil and gleaming in the sun, leaves the quay to begin its two-mile voyage upriver toward the temple of Luxor, Asru's husband lifts the smallest of their children on his shoulders. The pharaoh himself rides the gilded barge of Amun, making the ritual offerings. His queen stands proudly on the barge of the goddess Mut. And on the barge of Khons, the onlookers may even see the crown prince posing in full princely regalia. The crowds of onlookers move with the fleet, the children running ahead along the shore and the grown-ups calling out to their offspring to be careful. But everyone is in a holiday mood. And what evil can come to pass during the great festival of Amun?

That evening Asru and her family gather in the salon on the ground floor for a feast of roast duck, beef, bread and cakes, grapes, pomegranates, dates, figs, and honey. There is ample wine and beer with which to toast the pharaoh: May he live long and rule wisely. Perhaps a small orchestra of hired musicians accompanies the meal. When the day finally ends, the children fall asleep exhausted while their parents climb the stairs to the third-floor terrace to enjoy the cool night air and rehearse the wonderful events of the day.

All in all, Asru and Djedmaatesankh lived good lives in a pleasant place — that is, until their final illnesses. From the evidence, both must have been very sick women when they died. Although the CAT scan of Djed has revealed the agonizing cause of her death, we actually know more about Asru's medical condition, since we've been able to perform detailed analyses on samples of her tissue.

Because Asru lived much longer than Djed, quite possibly into her sixties according to the latest information, she could look back on a full life with satisfaction. That didn't make the pain of her final illness any less severe. She suffered from two parasitical diseases, strongylosis and schistosomiasis,

(Opposite) A guest who has just arrived at a banquet is adorned with a fragrant flower collar made of lotus petals. (Above) The Egyptians took for granted that they would need to beautify themselves in the next world. This jewel case and cosmetics container were found in a woman's tomb.

as well as from desert lung disease, osteoarthritis, a slipped disc, and, quite possibly, diabetes.

Thanks to the fascinating work that has been done in Toronto and Manchester on these two ancient women, I almost feel as if I know each of them personally. I would love to have sat down with both of them — when they were young and healthy — and talked about their lives, their families, and their world.

—Rosalie David

CHAPTER FIVE

ANCIENT GENES

THE 1999 REMAKE OF THE 1932 HORROR CLASSIC, *THE MUMMY*, OPENS WITH THE MURDER of Pharaoh Sethos I by his mistress and her lover, a high priest called Imhotep. After the royal mistress impales herself on her own dagger, Imhotep attempts to bring her back to life — an unforgivable sacrilege, for which he is punished by being mummified alive. His still-breathing body is wrapped in bandages, then placed in a coffin. Before the lid closes, his executioners unleash a horde of flesh-eating scarab beetles into his coffin. We are left to imagine the rest.

Flesh-eating scarabs may be a biological fiction — the scarab being a creature that consumes dung, not flesh — but this fiction is only one of many historical howlers in the movie. Imhotep, a name famous from the Old Kingdom (ca. 2686-ca. 2181 B.C.E.), was the architect who designed the first pyramid. No high priest of that name is known from the New Kingdom, more than a thousand years later, when Sethos I ruled. And as to the pyramids themselves, several are visible in the background, even though the movie opens in Thebes, more than five hundred kilometers south of the real pyramids. As for Sethos I, founder of the 19th Dynasty (the second of the New Kingdom), all evidence indicates that he died in his bed.

What's interesting about *The Mummy* isn't its ancient inaccuracies, but the basis of its box office success: it was one of the top-grossing films of 1999. For all the movie's spectacular special effects, its appeal, like that of its predecessors that form a lengthy lineage dating back to the 1932 original starring Boris Karloff, surely derives from our eternal fascination with the idea of rebirth. There is something irresistible about an ancient human being who comes back to life after three thousand years, no matter how impossibly far-fetched the idea.

But real science often makes better reading than science fiction. In 1985, Svante Pääbo, a Swedish molecular biologist working at the University of Uppsala, successfully extracted DNA from the 2,400-year-old mummy of a one-year-old Egyptian child. Recently, Pääbo analyzed the DNA of the Stone Age man dug out of a glacier in the Alps in 1991 in an attempt to track down traces of ancient viruses. If ancient viral DNA survives, then it may be possible to trace the evolution of a Stone

This pectoral shows the scarab beetle with wings extended, representing the sun god and resurrection. The association of the scarab with eternal life seems to have derived from the beetle's seemingly miraculous ability to be born spontaneously out of the ground. In another form, the heart scarab, a beetle-shaped amulet, was placed within a mummy's bandages over the heart to make sure that the heart did not testify against its owner at the judgment of truth.

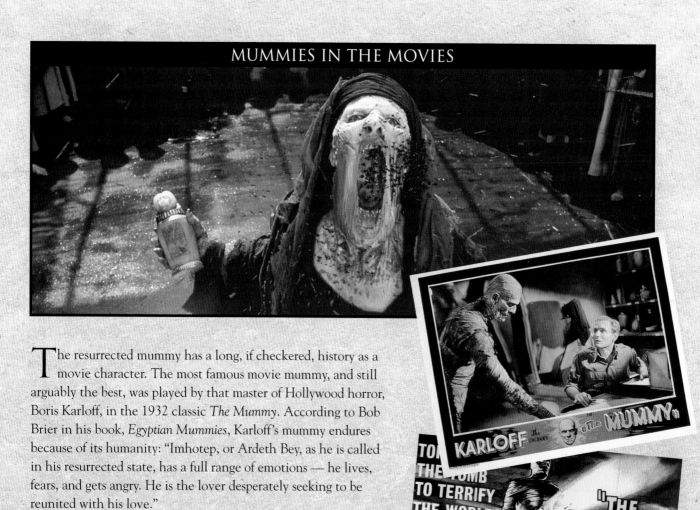

MUMMIES IN THE MOVIES

The resurrected mummy has a long, if checkered, history as a movie character. The most famous movie mummy, and still arguably the best, was played by that master of Hollywood horror, Boris Karloff, in the 1932 classic *The Mummy*. According to Bob Brier in his book, *Egyptian Mummies*, Karloff's mummy endures because of its humanity: "Imhotep, or Ardeth Bey, as he is called in his resurrected state, has a full range of emotions — he lives, fears, and gets angry. He is the lover desperately seeking to be reunited with his love."

In contrast to the 70 days it took to make an ancient mummy, Karloff's transformation from man to mummy took only eight hours. Once the wet cotton strips applied to his face had dried, they were covered with beauty mud, into which wrinkles were carved. The rest of his body was wrapped in linen. According to legend, the first time he appeared on the set in full mummy garb, the whole cast and crew let out a gasp.

The earliest cinematic mummy appeared in *The Mummy of King Ramses* in 1909. The most recent appeared in 1999's *The Mummy* (top), although its title character, also called Imhotep, completely lacks Karloff's human foibles. The genre perhaps reached its lowest ebb with *I Was a Teenage Mummy* in 1992. It enjoyed its heyday in the years following the Karloff classic in a series of films all made by Universal Studios: *The Mummy's Hand* (1940), *The Mummy's Tomb* (1942), *The Mummy's Ghost* (1944), and *The Mummy's Curse* (1945). In these films the mummy became the robot-like presence he remains to this day. Alas.

Age virus over the last five thousand years. Which brings our story back to Manchester, England.

By cloning mummy DNA, Svante Pääbo opened a new door to a fascinating area of mummy science: paleoepidemiology, or the study of how epidemic diseases have evolved since ancient times. Where an ancient disease still poses a major health problem, a study of how it has changed over several millennia could well lead to better modern treatments and even cures. The results of the mummy autopsies and endoscopies of the 1970s and 1980s proved that parasites ranging from tapeworms to malaria collectively posed the biggest health problem in the land of the pharaohs. One of the most common ancient diseases, which continues to afflict millions of contemporary Egyptians, goes by two modern names, bilharziasis or schistosomiasis. It can be treated and cured, but reinfection cannot be prevented.

Every time modern Egyptians come into contact with fresh water, they risk infection from one of two schistosome parasites that thrive in the Middle East. The eggs of the parasite hatch inside the bodies of waterborne snails, which release a swimming version of the larvae into the water. When these larvae come into contact with human skin, they penetrate via a hair follicle and immediately develop into worms. The infected person usually experiences a skin reaction sometimes referred to as "swimmer's itch." After a few days, the itch goes away — but the parasite doesn't.

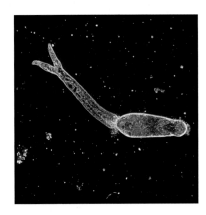

The tiny larval stage of the schistosome parasite swims invisibly in Egyptian waters.

The worm migrates through the bloodstream to the liver, where it copulates, then, depending on the species, takes up residence either in the intestines or the bladder, where it lays its eggs. If enough eggs accumulate and start to hatch, they will cause internal bleeding. As a result, blood will show up in the feces or the urine. Over time, a chronic schistosome infection will cause calcification of the bladder, fibrosis of the intestine, and scarring and cirrhosis of the liver. In the meantime, the sufferer will become seriously anemic and chronically fatigued. Schistosomiasis can also lead to heart disease — a swelling of the right ventricle related to damage to the pulmonary arteries. In rare cases, the condition can cause death. Regardless, it makes life extremely uncomfortable and difficult.

The parasite completes its lifecycle when stool or urine carrying its eggs is excreted into fresh water, where it seeks out its snail hosts and begins its journey again. Not surprisingly, modern Egyptian health authorities are anxious to find a solution to this debilitating problem.

EARLY IN 1996, ROSALIE DAVID RECEIVED A VISIT FROM DR. GEORGE CONTIS, PRESIDENT OF MEDICAL Service Corporation International of Arlington, Virginia. Dr. Contis's company, which specializes in setting up medical delivery systems in the developing world, was under contract with the Egyptian Ministry of Health to do a modern schistosomiasis study. Thanks to a personal interest in paleopathology, Contis knew about the Mummy Research Project. He proposed that the Manchester team conduct a study of ancient schistosomiasis that could be combined with the work his company was doing. To Rosalie, the idea represented a perfectly logical next step for the Mummy Project, and she readily agreed. Thus was hatched the Schistosomiasis in Ancient and Modern Egypt Project, a joint effort by the Manchester Mummy Project, the Egyptian Ministry of Health, and Medical Service Corporation International. It would be the first large-scale study of the evolution of a single disease over five thousand years.

*(Opposite) A modern Egyptian landscape looks little different from the land in ancient times, its single dominating feature the Nile.
(Above) One of the tiny snails that bring the schistosome parasite into contact with human hosts.*

To learn about the ancient form of the disease, the project needed Egyptian mummy tissue, lots of it — samples from as many mummies as possible. For researchers to have easy and consistent access, the samples needed to be stored in one place: a tissue bank. And so in 1997 the Manchester Mummy Tissue Bank was founded.

Locating every known mummy outside of Egypt is a daunting task. Fortunately for Patricia Lambert-Zazulak, the recently graduated Egyptologist with a background in radiography who took on the job of tracking every Egyptian mummy in the world, there was a firm base on which to build: the information collected in the 1980s for the Manchester Mummy Project's mummy data bank. This computerized mummy catalogue contained hundreds of entries that gave Lambert-Zazulak a start on a mailing list. Then she built on it by contacting thousands of other potential sources. But this was not the end of her work. Whereas the earlier effort had simply recorded where a mummy was and some information about it, she needed to persuade the owner to agree to donate mummy tissue to the tissue bank.

Lambert-Zazulak spent the better part of her first year creating a computerized database of potential contributors. At times she must have wondered why she'd spent all those hours studying the ancient links between medicine and religion for her Ph.D. thesis — "The Concepts of Healing in the Ancient Egyptian Context" — only to have her days filled with the pursuit of mummy parts. On the other hand, as she says now, "the remains we have are the product of the ancient Egyptians'

155

belief in the afterlife. So in a way each mummy is a physical manifestation of that religious belief."

What made a mummy suitable for the tissue bank? Any certifiable ancient Egyptian body or body part, embalmed or not, was welcome, but the more that was known about the source mummy — above all, a reasonably precise date of death — the more useful its tissue became. Ideally, the bank would include a range of samples from each of the main historical periods, going back to the Old Kingdom, so that the study would truly be able to track the disease's evolution. For each tissue sample in the bank, the database would include as much information as possible about the source mummy: photographs and results of any previous studies or scientific examinations.

The ideal deposit in the Mummy Tissue Bank consisted of 1 to 2 grams of dry tissue from several uncontaminated body sites, including, if possible, a hair sample. Since schistosomiasis eggs tend to gather in the liver, the bladder, and the intestines, samples from these organs were particularly welcome.

But in 1997, as the schistosomiasis study was getting underway, accumulating a large bank of tissue samples was the least of the project's problems. Obviously, you can't compare an ancient disease with its modern form if you can't find it. With only a few tiny tissue fragments per mummy in the bank, the Manchester team had to come up with a reliable method — the scientific term is "protocol" — for locating and identifying schistosomiasis in very small samples of ancient remains. This task fell to a second Patricia from Manchester, a Ph.D. student named Patricia Rutherford.

Patricia Lambert-Zazulak places a sample in Manchester's Mummy Tissue Bank. In this simple storage cupboard within the museum's Mummy Store rest tissue samples representing a growing number of Egyptian mummies from around the world.

TRICIA RUTHERFORD IS A DISEASE DETECTIVE, A MOLECULAR BIOLOGIST who specializes in immunocytochemistry — a marriage of microscopy and immunology that studies the chemical changes in disease-infected cells. She is also one of the first graduates of Manchester's new M.Sc. in Biomedical and Forensic Studies in Egyptology, Rosalie David's latest brainchild. When Tricia began her work on the Schistosomiasis Project, she couldn't even be sure that enough of the tissue samples would be well enough preserved for her to consistently find the evidence she needed. Unlike the teams of scientists who performed the autopsies of PUM-II, Nakht, Mummy 1770, and the other Egyptian mummies that turned up evidence of schistosomiasis, Tricia did not have as much raw material (mummy tissue) to work with. She had to come up with a practical, repeatable, relatively inexpensive protocol that would detect schistosomiasis in tiny fragments of ancient mummy. As far as she and Rosalie knew, Tricia would be the only researcher in the world studying schistosomiasis in ancient tissue.

Both species of the schistosome parasite that infect modern Egyptians, S. *mansoni* and S. *haematobium*, are easy to diagnose in living people, since their eggs have distinctive shapes when examined under a microscope. In a fragment of ancient tissue, however, all that may remain is a microscopic shard of the egg or the worm. So Tricia had to come up with a way of tracking even a trace of the ancient parasite.

In living tissue, the simplest way of inferring the presence of a disease is to look for its antibody — the custom-designed molecules that our bodies manufacture to fight off disease. Every foreign entity, or antigen, that invades the human body stimulates the creation of a unique antibody — an amalgam of proteins that has rapidly modified itself to fit the antigen's chemical signature, in Tricia's words, "like lock and key," stopping the invader in its tracks. If the body produces enough of these antibodies quickly enough, they will defeat the disease. After the disease is vanquished, its unique antibodies remain, ready to fend off the next attack by a similar invader.

Research suggests, however, that antigens are hardier than antibodies, and therefore more likely to survive in ancient tissue. So Tricia decided to target the schistosome antigen instead of looking for its antibodies. To do so meant she would have to come up with a reliable way of isolating any trace of the parasite — either worm or egg — left in ancient tissue. The process took a year.

Her first step was to find the perfect antiserum. An antiserum contains antibodies that will bind to specific antigen sites called epitopes. Thus, if an antiserum for the schistosome parasite is added to tissue containing either a dead or a living form of the parasite, the antibodies in the antiserum will bind to these antigens. Once the tissue is thoroughly washed, the researcher can be confident that only the antibodies that have formed chemical bonds with the antigen will remain. For Tricia, the disease detective, the antibodies would act like bloodhounds that unerringly track down a suspect.

The final step in the detection process is called tissue staining. Here, a second set of new trackers enters the hunt — molecular tags that will bind with a specific antibody. Depending on the tag chosen, it will show up under the microscope in one of several colors.

In the histology lab on the third floor of the Stopford Building, which houses the research labs for the University of Manchester's Medical School and its School of Biological Sciences, Tricia Rutherford soon became known as the Mummy Lady. The other researchers in the lab tended to be doctors studying wound healing so as to develop better techniques for plastic surgery. Some were physicians who'd returned to school for advanced degrees; they would be there for while, then move on.

The consistent presence was Frank Barnett, a veteran histologist with 40 years' experience. Frank, who knew as much about sectioning and staining tissue as anyone in England, ruled the lab with friendly seniority. Those who didn't want to listen to classical music on BBC Radio 3 wore headphones. Frank had formerly played the cornet in a brass band and enjoyed challenging his colleagues to "name that composer." Whenever Tricia was having trouble with her work, she turned to Barnett for advice. In the fall of 1997, as she was beginning her study, she turned to him often.

Tricia's first job was to find the right antiserum. She began by testing a series of antisera extracted from rabbits that had been infected with *S. mansoni*. Her test tissue came from mouse livers infected with the same species of the parasite. In theory, the antibodies in the serum would bind with the epitope sites on the antigens of the parasite in the mouse livers. They did, beautifully. Next, Tricia tried the same antiserum on older tissue: samples from the bladder of an Egyptian who had died about 50 years before and whose infected bladder had been preserved in wax. Once again, the antibodies bound to the schistosome antigen epitopes, and the tissue stained beautifully. Moreover, since this 50-year-old tissue was infected with the second parasite species on her most-wanted list, *S. haematobium*, Tricia now knew that her antiserum worked on both the schistosome species alive and well in Egypt today. She had developed a sure-fire method of detecting the disease in modern tissue.

Now she was ready to test her protocol on ancient bodies. For her initial experiments, she used tissue from Mummy 1766 in the Manchester Museum collection, an anonymous woman who had lived sometime during the first or second centuries C.E., during the period when Egypt belonged to the Roman Empire. Mummy 1766 immediately became known as the Test Case Mummy. Since this mummy was still wrapped in bandages that had been coated in resin and had a painted piece of cartonnage over her face and upper body, the tissue samples were extracted by means of carefully targeted endoscopy, proving once again the value of this technique in mummy research. The samples included some pieces of calcified bladder, a condition that often results from infection by *S. haematobium*.

Before you can cut a slice of ancient mummy tissue, it must be rehydrated, or softened. The better the quality of the softened tissue, the thinner the cross-section that can be cut. The thinner the cross-section, the more clearly it will tell its story under the microscope. But as many researchers before Tricia Rutherford had discovered, mummy tissue is fiendishly difficult to work with. "If you've seen mummy tissue, you'll know what it's like — either leathery or very brittle and crumbly," she says. "And some of it's got lots of sand in it. Getting a protocol that would work was a nightmare."

She spent months on the problem, trying every conceivable softening solution. For her purposes, the various versions of Ruffer's Solution now in use didn't measure up. In the end, ordinary unscented fabric softener worked best. (The scent added to commercial fabric softeners could interfere with molecular reactions.) She's been using it ever since.

At this stage in her research, Tricia also had to figure out a way to deal with the sand — silica — that so often impregnated the tissue, including tissue from a mummy's viscera. Even using the finest cutting tool at her disposal, a diamond knife, she had trouble with the tissue from the Test Case Mummy, and when the work was successful, the wear and tear on this expensive piece of

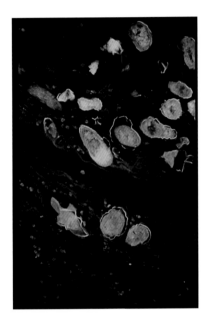

Patricia Rutherford (right) examines 50-year-old bladder tissue beneath a fluorescent microscope. The green shapes visible here are schistosome eggs.

equipment was considerable. She realized she had to get rid of the sand before sectioning.

After she'd tried numerous alternatives, Frank suggested hydrofluoric acid, an extremely dangerous and highly toxic substance — even its fumes can cause burns — that dissolves silica. Hydrofluoric acid is so deadly that a tiny amount can kill you. Tricia took the tissue samples to her husband's chemical plant, where she could experiment in the most controlled environment possible. Her idea was to find a solution of the acid strong enough to dissolve the sand but weak enough not to harm the tissue. She did.

At long last, after a year of experimentation, of false starts and wrong turns, she had achieved her initial goal: excellent sections of mummy tissue as thin as 2 microns, thinner than the thinnest piece of tissue paper. Finally, she was ready to stain some of the bladder tissue from Mummy 1766. Because the bladder had calcified, she was reasonably confident that this mummy had schistosomiasis.

Compared to the seemingly endless process of perfecting the protocol, trying it out on the Test Case Mummy went without a hitch. Tricia sectioned some bladder tissue, added some antiserum to each section, then left everything in the lab fridge to incubate overnight. The next day, she stained the samples with a chemical that carried a colored fluorescent tag, then mounted and fixed them on glass slides, and left them in the freezer to set overnight.

On the morning of the third day, she took her slides to the microscope room. This would be the final test of her protocol. She placed the first slide under a fluorescent microscope equipped with a digital camera. She bent over to peer through the eyepiece and let out an exclamation of delight. Several eggs of S. *haematobium* gleamed apple-green before her eyes. She snapped a digital photo. It was difficult not to do a jig around the lab.

Patricia Rutherford had just made a breakthrough for mummy science. She had developed a fool-proof method for tracking down an ancient disease in ancient tissue. The first person she called with the good news was Rosalie David.

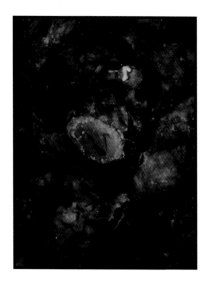

Under Tricia Rutherford's fluorescent microscope, schistosome eggs gleam apple-green. Rutherford's development of a reliable protocol for identifying the parasite in ancient tissue brought the Schistosomiasis Project one step closer to its goal of tracing the development of the disease.

BY THE SPRING OF 2000, AS THIS BOOK WAS GOING TO press, Rosalie David had good reason to be pleased with the progress of the Schistosomiasis Project. The Mummy Tissue Bank had received tissue deposits from more than three hundred mummies residing in places as far-flung as Australia. Of these, Tricia Rutherford had studied tissue from more than 25 and discovered one or the other species of schistosome parasite in 30 percent of them. In the next few years, Manchester hopes to have more than a thousand mummies represented in its Tissue Bank, all of which will be tested in time, for schistosomiasis. But the bank is still waiting for deposits from some of the most famous mummies in the world of paleopathology, including PUM-II and Nakht, who definitely carried schistosomiasis. These and all the mummies represented in the bank will be available to any reputable researcher in the world who wants to study ancient tissue.

As for the Schistosomiasis Project, it has already entered a new and even more fascinating phase — DNA research. Soon after her initial success, Tricia Rutherford began extracting DNA from both *S. haematobium* and *S. mansoni*. When enough DNA has been gathered, she and colleagues in England and Egypt will be able to set the ancient and modern forms of the parasite side by side and compare them gene for gene. Perhaps they will discover distinct evolutionary differences, which may point the way to modern treatments and feed into our growing knowledge of how diseases evolve.

Elsewhere in Manchester, researchers at the Christie Hospital are busy investigating a single schistosome gene they believe may be connected to bladder cancer, which many people who suffer from schistosomiasis eventually develop. This is just one example of the myriad possible spin-offs from the type of work Tricia Rutherford is doing.

The Schistosomiasis Project is only the first of a planned series of studies of diseases over time. Next on the list at Manchester is malaria, a mosquito-borne parasitical disease which has been discovered in many Egyptian mummies and which is a major health problem in Egypt and elsewhere today.

Mummy science has made amazing strides since the pioneering autopsies of the early 1970s. Gene cloning will likely never bring an ancient mummy back to life, except in some Hollywood fantasy, but scientific methods have brought us much closer to the mummy's world. At the beginning of a new millennium, the modern science of paleopathology is delving into the secrets of life itself.

ANCIENT MALARIA

The next area of investigation for the Manchester Mummy Project will be malaria in its ancient and modern forms. Malaria remains one of the most widespread and troublesome diseases of the tropical and subtropical worlds. More than 200 million cases occur every year. There are four strains of malaria, all protozoa belonging to the *Plasmodium* family, all borne by mosquitoes which deposit the parasite in human blood through their bite. In Egypt, the most common form is *P. falciparum*. Ancient medical papyri make no mention of malaria symptoms — recurring fevers every four days — but there seems little doubt the disease was endemic. In 1994, a series of mummies dating from pre-dynastic times to the Roman period all tested positive for the *P. falciparum* antigen. And we know from the detailed autopsy of Nakht that malaria was almost certainly one of his many complaints. Advances in mummy science may someday help cure another scourge, both historic and contemporary.

A CONVERSATION WITH SETHOS I

No visitor to Egypt can fail to be impressed by the magnificent vestiges of the reign of Ramesses II, perhaps the most famous of all the pharaohs. The massive monuments he built to his own memory inspired Shelley's poem that begins, "My name is Ozymandias, king of kings: / Look on my works, ye Mighty and despair!" These works seem to be everywhere. Ramesses reigned so long — 66 years — and ruled over an Egypt so rich and so powerful that he was able to leave an unmatched physical legacy of temples and monuments. (It sometimes seems that every pharaoh sought to outbuild his predecessors, but Ramesses outbuilt them all.)

If you look more closely at what Ramesses built, however, you will discover it often stands on his father's foundations — both literally and

metaphorically. For example, his great mortuary temple on the west bank of the Nile at Thebes — the Ramesseum — was carefully aligned with a nearby temple built by Ramesses' father, Sethos I, at Gurna. The remains can still be seen, and its construction was closely based on the plan of that temple. Only at Abydos, however, where Sethos I built his own mortuary temple — the most beautiful surviving temple in Egypt — do his works tower over those of his son and heir. During the spring I spent at Abydos when I was in my 20s, I began to feel as though I was getting to know personally this less famous, but no less great, pharaoh, the true founder of the 19th Dynasty (1320-1200 B.C.E.).

Sethos I was in his late 20s when he inherited the realm from his father, Ramesses I, who had died barely a year after taking office. Fortunately for Sethos, Egypt was already on the road to

(Above) His body may have shrunk, but the face of Sethos I remains hauntingly lifelike. Not so the badly damaged remains of one of his wooden coffins (opposite) — of whose original decoration only the eyes remain. The sketched features visible today were added by much later artists, long after his tomb had been plundered.

recovery after the troubled tenure of Akhenaten and the weak kingship of Tutankhamen. The boy king had been succeeded by the capable general Haremhab, who had restored much of Egypt's former glory. Upon assuming the throne, Sethos moved decisively to build on Haremhab's legacy.

He came from a line of soldiers, and the early years of his reign were filled with military campaigns into the areas of modern Israel, Palestine, and Syria, where he reasserted traditional Egyptian control. We can get a sense of his warlike face from an inscription commemorating his first campaign into Canaan carved on a wall of the great hypostyle hall — or hall supported by columns — of his temple at Karnak.

"Now as for this goodly god [the king], he exults at beginning the battle, he delights to enter into it; his heart is gratified at the sight of blood. He lops off the heads of the dissidents. More than the day of rejoicing he loves the moment of crushing [the foe]. His majesty slays them at one stroke — he leaves them no heirs, and who[ever] escapes his hand is brought prisoner to Egypt."

War excursions took up at most only a few summer months. However, during the rest of the year, the pharaoh held court in the ancient capital of Memphis (near modern-day Cairo), relaxed at his summer palace in the eastern delta, or retreated south to his winter residence in Thebes, where he could participate in the great Festival of Opet. With him traveled his great wife, Queen Tuy, as well as his lesser wives and the concubines of the royal harem. And wherever he went, Sethos was accompanied by his retinue of advisers, officials, and well-bred attendants, known as royal cupbearers.

I like to envision him at his lovely summer palace, at the place that would later become his son's personal capital, Pi-Ramesses, receiving tribute from his Asian vassals and undoubtedly feeling rather pleased with himself. The crown prince Ramesses had proved his mettle in battle early in Sethos' reign and was looking every inch the worthy successor. From a scribal exercise of the era — a text copied by students aspiring to join this educated elite — we get a glimpse of the opulence of pharaonic living:

"Get on with having everything ready for the Pharaoh's [arrival]. . . Have made [ready] 100 ring-stands for bouquets of flowers, 500 food baskets.

A wall painting from the tomb of Sethos I depicts a scene from the Book of Gates. *A boat carries the sun god on his 12-hour journey through the world of darkness.*

In profile, the face of the
pharaoh, who probably
died in his 40s, could be
that of a king who
has just fallen asleep
and will soon awake to
resume his royal duties.

Food-stuff, list, to be prepared: 1,000 loaves of fine flour; ... 10,000 ibshet-biscuits; 2,000 tjet-loaves; ... Cakes, 100 baskets, ... 70 dishes, ... 2,000 measures. ... Dried meat, 100 baskets at 300 cuts ... Milk, 60 measures; cream, 90 measures; carob beans, 30 bowls. Grapes, 50 sacks; pomegranates, 60 sacks; figs, 300 strings and 20 baskets. ... "

At his summer palace, as at Memphis, the pharaoh's life alternated between affairs of state and lavish indulgences. Official records of his reign provide few hints about his private life, but we can assume that he doted on his grandchildren. And it appears that he was devoted to his loyal wife, Queen Tuy, who seems to have been a model consort. Indeed, life was good as Sethos I entered the 11th year of his reign. His borders were secure, his country united and prosperous. Then, suddenly, in the prime of life, he fell ill and very quickly died.

After the ritual 70 days of preparation, his elaborately mummified body made the long journey up the Nile to Thebes, where it was borne in state to the tomb prepared for it in the Valley of the Kings, perhaps the most beautiful tomb ever built. All Thebes watched the cortège as it made its progress from the river toward the hills to the west. The great sarcophagus was laid in the burial chamber, the tomb doors sealed. Sethos' voyage to the afterlife had begun.

Of all the royal mummies in the Cairo Museum, the mummy of Sethos is perhaps the most memorable. It exudes such serenity and power — as if the pharaoh has just fallen asleep — and it is one of the supreme examples of the embalmer's art. His head is one of the best preserved and most lifelike. If you compare its profile with a profile from the Abydos reliefs, you

can see that they are one and the same person.

Unfortunately, when Sethos was discovered among the great cache of royal mummies at Deir el Bahari in 1881, his head and body had been separated and his body was badly damaged, undoubtedly by the plunderers of his original tomb. (His and the other mummies in the cache were moved to a group tomb during the 21st Dynasty (ca. 1089-945 B.C.E.) to protect them from further damage by tomb robbers.) Then, in the 19th century, Gaston Maspero didn't treat him with much respect. In June 1886 he unwrapped Sethos and two other pharaohs from the same cache in a single day.

Since then, the only scientific analysis of the mummy of Sethos I has come in the form of X-rays taken in the late 1960s by a team from the University of Michigan's School of Dentistry, led by James Harris and Kent Weeks. Their X-rays showed that Sethos was buried with his arms crossed over his chest and his hands open, a pose that became standard for royal males. The X-rays also indicated that Sethos died sometime between the ages of 35 and 40, somewhat younger than previously believed. His teeth show the typical wear and tear for a person of his age but no sign of serious dental disease. Like many mummies, royal or otherwise, he had arteriosclerosis, proof that hardening of the arteries was no respecter of class distinctions.

Until scientists are permitted to study Sethos I in more detail, we won't know more about how he died. But even more than the face of his famous son, it is the face of Sethos I that represents for me ancient Egypt at its most serene and self-assured.

—*Rosalie David*

167

CHAPTER SIX

CONVERSATIONS WITH MUMMIES

EGYPTIAN PALEOPATHOLOGY, MUMMY SCIENCE, IS ABOUT LIFE: LIFE IN ANCIENT TIMES AND LIFE today. The study of ancient remains is a two-way conversation: they speak to us; we speak to them. From studying the evidence of disease, we can learn much about the world of the pharaohs. By comparing our bodies with theirs, we can make discoveries relevant to our modern selves. Mummy science historian Bob Brier puts it nicely: "We study paleopathology for two reasons. One is, of course, to learn more about the daily life of the ancient Egyptians, but the other is to learn more about us. If you can track the progress of a disease from ancient times to modern, then you've got a better chance of predicting new diseases and how they're going to develop."

No amount of scientific investigation, however, can complete our unfinished portrait of the ancient Egyptians. Our version of their world will always be a mixture of fact and fancy — educated guesswork — where the speculation far outweighs the certainty. But each new piece of information — the discovery that ancient Egyptians got arthritis or suffered from tuberculosis — brings the partial portrait slightly more into focus and improves our chances of guessing right. Already, mummy science has added enormously to our understanding of the texture of ancient life in the Valley of the Nile. But despite the amazing advances of recent years, this dialogue is still in its early stages. In the coming decades, surprising discoveries may emerge from our ongoing conversations with mummies.

The picture we have so far is sharply at odds with much of the physical evidence — the art and literature — that has survived from ancient Egypt. The literature is generally so positive in tone that Egyptologists refer to the notable exception, dating back to the time of troubles called the First Intermediate Period, as the Pessimistic Literature.

These lovely alabaster stoppers graced the four jars in the canopic chest of Tutankhamen, which contained the pharaoh's embalmed organs. The faces depict the boy king himself. The vulture and the cobra in his headdress represent Nekbet, goddess of Upper Egypt, and Wadjet, goddess of lower Egypt, ancient symbols of the Two Lands.

The Egyptians' conception of the afterlife is a glowing one — and striking for its similarity to their living world. The fields of heaven are perfect replicas of the fields of grain that stretched along the banks of the Nile. The walled orchards and gardens of the next world are just like the enclosed orchards and gardens that provided fruits and vegetables year round on earth. On coffins and on the walls of tombs, funerary artists depicted the life to come in gorgeous detail. It differs from mortal life in only one important detail: the nature of work. The fields must still be tilled, the crops harvested, the crafts created, but now the hard labor is performed by magical servants called *ushabtis*, whose toil leaves the reborn with time for leisure.

The ancient Egyptians could imagine nothing better than a continuation of their life on earth — without the daily toil. Perhaps we shouldn't be surprised at this attitude, given the apparent stability and plenty of pharaonic civilization during almost three millennia. With the exception of relatively brief periods of turmoil, possibly connected to periods of decreased food production, ancient Egypt seems to represent in many ways a model society. Most people had a job, a place to live, and enough to eat. The overwhelming impression one gains from reading the surviving literature is of a people happy with its lot and optimistic about the future.

How, then, do we reconcile the Egyptians' own conception of their lives as basically good and happy with the disease-ridden condition of their mummified remains? The mummy autopsies, whether of a person young or old, invariably reveal traces of many different debilitating diseases. The ancient Egyptians were infested with parasites ranging from large tapeworms to microscopic schistosome eggs. An adult Egyptian jaw without teeth worn to the pulp and serious dental disease was a rarity. Desert lung disease and black lung disease were epidemic; malaria was probably widespread. Smallpox and other infectious diseases, among them tuberculosis, periodically ravaged the population. The more one examines the physical evidence, the more difficult it becomes to imagine that there were any adults in ancient Egypt who were free of chronic pain, who were not often too ill to work. Yet they built the pyramids, erected the magnificent temple of Queen Hatshepsut at Thebes, and created the timeless wall carvings inside the temple of Sethos I at Abydos.

I T IS DIFFICULT FOR PEOPLE AT THE TURN OF THE 20TH CENTURY TO IMAGINE LIVING WITHOUT VACCINES, antibiotics, and modern dentistry. Yet we have only to consider the circumstances of daily life in parts of the developing world today to gain some insight into the state of health in ancient Egypt. An ancient Egyptian who lived to the age of 30 had reached the end of his society's average lifespan, which was no different from that of a European peasant in the Middle Ages. Medical progress between those eras was slow. More medical advances have been made in the last hundred years than in the previous five millennia.

DOCTORING IN THE LAND OF THE PHARAOHS

What we know of ancient Egyptian medical practice has been gleaned from a few surviving depictions of doctors at work and the fragmentary written record provided by the so-called medical papyri. We possess but a fraction of what must have been an extensive library of Egyptian medical texts. Many, particularly those of later periods, are mostly compendiums of spells. But in a few cases, the papyri give us a tantalizing glimpse into what was undoubtedly the first systematic practice of medicine in the history of civilization. The most important of these, the Edwin Smith Papyrus, was purchased in 1862 by an American then living in Luxor. By the style of writing, it can be dated to around 1550 B.C.E.,

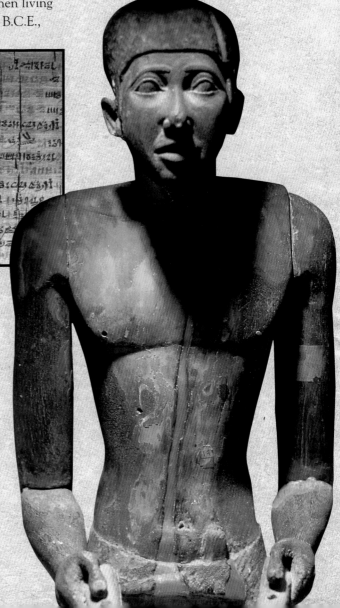

This wooden statue from Saqqara may represent Imhotep, the most accomplished commoner in ancient history. Besides designing the first pyramid, he was revered as the quintessential doctor, the father of Egyptian medicine.

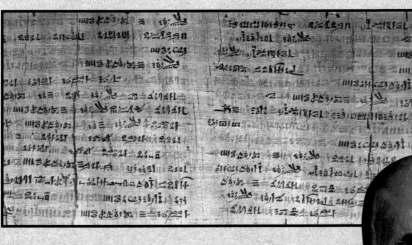

but, like a number of other medical papyri, it appears to be a copy of a much earlier manuscript, probably a thousand years older. It thus represents a snapshot of medical practice in the Old Kingdom. According to John F. Nunn in his definitive book *Ancient Egyptian Medicine*, this papyrus is "remarkably free of magic." As an example he cites Case 16, instructions for treating a split in the cheek: "If you examine a man having a slit in his cheek and you find that there is swelling, raised and red, on the outside. … You should bandage it with fresh meat [on] the first day. His treatment is sitting until his swelling is reduced. Afterwards you should treat it [with] grease, honey and a pad every day until he is well."

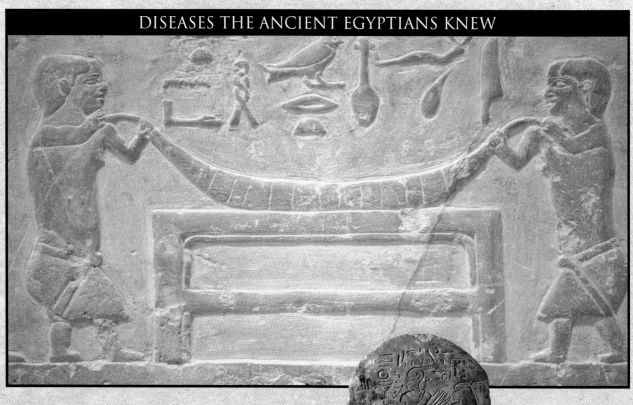

Unaware of the microscopic causes of many diseases, Egyptian doctors could deal only with their symptoms. Thus, malarial fever would have been treated, but no attempt made to eradicate the mosquito that bore the parasite. But when it came to setting a fracture or dressing a wound, Egyptian medicine was often quite practical. The Egyptians also had various remedies, including pomegranate and wormwood, for larger parasites that would have been visible in a person's stool. These would actually have done some good. In general, however, Egyptian drug therapy was closer to 18th-century European medical practice than to practice in the 20th century. Here, from the Brooklyn papyrus, is an ancient remedy for snakebite: "Onion, ground finely in beer. Eat and spit out for one day. Then apply it to the bite." Natron, the salt compound used in mummification was also applied to wounds to reduce infection.

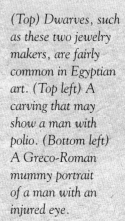

(Top) Dwarves, such as these two jewelry makers, are fairly common in Egyptian art. (Top left) A carving that may show a man with polio. (Bottom left) A Greco-Roman mummy portrait of a man with an injured eye.

Chronic disease was part of the fabric of daily life in ancient Egypt, as it was throughout the world until the 19th century — so much so, that some conditions we would call illnesses the ancients thought of as normal. Take bilharzia (schistosomiasis), for example. This parasitical disease was likely so epidemic in ancient Egypt that by the time boys reached puberty, they generally passed blood in their urine. The culprit, unknown to ancient Egyptian medicine, was the schistosome parasite, which causes internal bleeding when it infects the bladder. But to the Egyptian eye, both boys and girls appeared to menstruate.

Ancient Egyptian medicine lacks a term for anemia, the inevitable side effect of chronic schistosomiasis and other parasitic infestations. Nonetheless the ancient Egyptians suffered from the condition and the chronic fatigue that accompanies it. Does this mean that they were always sluggish, constantly in need of sleep? Nothing in their tales of war and peace, of battles won and great monuments built, suggests a civilization that lacked energy or drive. Perhaps their bodies had found ways to adapt, to co-exist with parasites in ways our vaccinated and frequently overmedicated bodies would be unable to do. In modern Egypt, for example, there is some evidence that not all those exposed to schistosome parasites develop the disease. Somehow they have become immune.

Proof that the Egyptians did not recognize many of the diseases from which they suffered can be gleaned from the medical papyri, the surviving written evidence of their medical practice. Only a precious few of these medical texts, handwritten on papyrus, have survived, some in frustratingly fragmentary form. They date from the Middle Kingdom (1991-1786 B.C.E.) or later, but usually seem to be copies made from earlier texts going back to the Old Kingdom (ca. 2686-2181 B.C.E.). The world's oldest written record of systematic medical practice, they are surprisingly practical for an age when doctoring combined rational treatment with magic and superstition.

The medical papyri seem most practical when they are describing treatments for physical trauma — a blow to the head, a broken leg, a scorpion sting — ailments whose cause is clear and symptoms obvious. They are less sure footed when dealing with infectious diseases. Not understanding the cause of these illnesses, Egyptian doctors often resorted to folk remedies, as well as magic spells and other superstitious practices.

IF MUMMY SCIENCE HAS BROUGHT US CLOSER TO THE WORLD OF THE ANCIENT EGYPTIANS, IT HAS ALSO allowed us to get to know a few individuals as well as it is possible to know a person who existed two or more thousand years ago. The all-conquering pharaoh Ramesses II becomes frailly human when we can reconstruct his face and identify the many diseases that plagued his old age. The boy weaver Nakht becomes more than an ancient statistic when we examine his stunted body, with its evidence of famine, and discover the particles of red granite in his lungs, suggesting that he must

THE VALLEY OF THE GILDED MUMMIES

As has happened so often in the annals of Egyptology, this great discovery occurred almost by accident. In 1996, near the verdant Bahariya Oasis in the Western Desert nearly 400 kilometers southwest of Cairo, a donkey stumbled into a depression in the ground. The animal belonged to an antiquities guard at the nearby Temple of Alexander the Great. The guard dug the sand away to free his donkey's hoof and discovered that the beast had broken through the roof of a deep cavity in the sandstone beneath the desert. He climbed inside and found himself face to face with a mummy. This was the first find in what would soon

(Above left) Two alcoves within an exposed tomb reveal their stash of mummies. (Above right) A view of the Bahariya Oasis. (Below right) Archeologists from the Egyptian Antiquities Service examine a tomb excavated in March 1998.

come to be known as the Valley of the Golden Mummies, a Greco-Roman burial ground of 200 tombs containing the remains of an estimated 10,000 people who lived in the first few centuries of the Common Era. If this estimate is correct, the Bahariya necropolis holds the greatest concentration of Egyptian mummies ever discovered.

In the late spring of 1999, front pages around the world trumpeted the spectacular finds from the four family tombs explored so far, each containing as many as 50 mummies apparently belonging to the same family. In one of these four tombs, Tomb 54, the Egyptian team of archeologists found 43 beautifully decorated mummies, their cartonnage face masks and aprons covered with gold leaf. These gilded mummies clearly belonged to persons of great wealth and high status, the most important being the mummy of a man wearing a cobra crown associated with the god Horus. In earlier times, such a headdress would have been reserved for members of the royal family. But by this period, it undoubtedly indicated a high official or wealthy landowner.

To the mummy scientist, however, the bodies within these gorgeous casings were the real find, a rare chance to examine and analyze a large number of people from the same family and presumably representing several generations. The work of these scientists, combined with the discoveries of the more traditional archeologists at work in the valley, will open a door into the last great era of ancient Egyptian life, just before Christ displaced Osiris and the rest of the ancient pantheon.

(Above left and right) Gilded mummies from tomb 54. (Opposite) The gilded face and cobra headdress mark this as a person of the highest status. (Below) A female mummy head (left) and three views of the same male mummy head. Archeologists believe that the tombs were placed at Bahariya because of its proximity to the Temple of Alexander the Great, who had adopted the sensible policy of turning himself into an Egyptian deity following his conquest of Egypt.

have done something to earn a sentence of hard labor. And the gorgeous cartonnage coffin of Djedmaatesankh, with its ritual invocation of a happy afterlife, becomes achingly poignant when we use the three-dimensional X-ray vision of a CAT scanner and discover the painful illness that must have afflicted Djed's final days.

Mummy science has also opened the door to a broader understanding of ancient Egyptian society. But there is much work to be done, both in re-examining the royal mummies with the latest methods and in investigating the many new mummies being discovered every year. Eventually, one hopes, the entire collection of mummies in the Cairo Museum will be analyzed for evidence of disease — information that may finally allow us to generalize about the lifestyle-related distinctions between the health of the aristocracy, the middle class, and the working class.

If the Egyptian authorities allow researchers to undertake medical and genetic analysis of the bodies of the pharaohs, the royal family tree will recover missing branches. For example, is the mummy known as "The Elder Lady" really that of Queen Tiyi, wife of Amenhotep II of the 18th Dynasty?

And what of the most recently uncovered royal remains, those buried in Tomb KV5 in the Valley of the Kings? Discovered by American Egyptologist Kent R. Weeks in 1989, this tomb was built during the reign of Ramesses the Great and may have been the burial place for some of his sons. Perhaps DNA analysis could confirm whether any of the mummy remains in KV5 are really related to Ramesses II.

THE LOST SONS OF RAMESSES II

In the Valley of the Kings, so exhaustively scoured by generations of Egyptologists, how can a tomb be lost? Yet since this famous necropolis was first excavated in the 19th century, a number of its tombs have gone missing, their entrances buried beneath debris from flash floods or adjacent excavations. One of them was a tomb designated KV5. It was first uncovered by an Englishman named James Burton in 1825. Discovering no objects of interest in the first few chambers of the tomb, he abandoned his excavation. The tomb was briefly investigated once again in 1902 by Howard Carter. Believing it to be a small tomb of little importance, Carter reburied the entrance and continued his exploration elsewhere in the Valley.

When Egyptologist Kent Weeks rediscovered KV5 in the summer of 1989, he was excited to note the royal cartouche of Ramesses II above its entranceway, but had no inkling of what he would find within. Carved reliefs in the first chambers seemed to suggest the tomb had once contained the remains of several of the 30-odd sons of Ramesses II, who outlived most of his progeny. With each year of excavation, the tomb grew in size and complexity until Weeks could state that it was "the largest tomb ever found in the valley, that its plan was unique, and that it apparently functioned as a family mausoleum for several sons of Ramesses II." Not until the autumn of 1997, however, nearly nine years after excavations began, did Weeks and his team uncover the first human remains. To date, parts of four mummies have been found, including one complete skeleton. But are these remains really the sons of Egypt's most famous pharaoh? And do more sons lie within the tomb's as-yet-unexcavated chambers?

(Top and above) Part of the excavated KV5 tomb complex, which contains 150 corridors and chambers. Tons of debris deposited by centuries of flash floods had to be removed before Weeks and his team could explore the tomb. (Right) This skeleton of an as-yet-unidentified adult male may be that of one of the sons of Ramesses the Great.

Beyond articulating the pharaonic family tree, DNA analysis of Egyptian mummies may actually answer a question that has fascinated Egyptologists and anthropologists for as long as they have been studying ancient Egypt: Where did the ancient Egyptians come from? Elliot Smith helped make his reputation by theorizing that the rise of the Old Kingdom coincided with the arrival in the Nile Valley of the "pharaonic race," a conquering people probably of Caucasian origin who transformed a Stone Age society into a great civilization virtually overnight. Smith's far-fetched hypothesis is now regarded as racist as well as wrong-headed, and it is now believed that the indigenous neolithic population of Egypt were the authors of this great civilization.

Svante Pääbo, the Swedish researcher who in 1985 became the first to clone mummy DNA, hopes to help confirm this modern theory. Pääbo has become one of the leading exponents of the study of the evolution of ancient DNA — or "molecular archeology." The DNA that survives best in ancient tissue comes from tiny energy factories inside each cell, called mitochondria. Because there are many mitochondria in each cell, but only one nucleus, fragments of mitochondrial DNA are much more likely to survive.

On an 18th-Dynasty mummy case, the face of Ahmose Merit-Amon seems to contemplate eternity.

Even better for the molecular archeologist, mitochondrial DNA evolves much more rapidly than the DNA found in a cell's nucleus and therefore "accumulates changes fast enough to allow differences to be observed over the short time period during which modern humans have differentiated," says Pääbo. What's more, mitochondrial DNA is maternally inherited — it carries only the characteristics of the mother — which means that paternal DNA doesn't get mixed in and interfere with the results. In essence, the technique Pääbo and others are developing permits them to create a molecular family tree for an entire population by connecting generations through maternal lines.

According to Pääbo, we now have the means by which "DNA sequences can be generated on a large scale from [ancient] populations. This allows a reconstruction of the history of the populations with the highest resolution attainable for molecular data." Molecular biologists working in close collaboration with archeologists, he says, "will eventually shed new light on the population history of the Nile Valley as well as other regions of the world."

AS MUCH AS MUMMY SCIENCE HAS TAUGHT US ABOUT THE REALITIES OF LIFE IN ANCIENT EGYPT, it promises to deliver equally great gifts of knowledge about ourselves and our world. This is the other half of the conversation, exemplified by the explorations of Rosalie David and her colleagues in Manchester. At the forefront of their work is the Schistosomiasis in Ancient and Modern Egypt Project, which aims to find more effective ways of treating the parasitical

scourge of the contemporary Nile Valley. The next study, of malaria, is already in its formative stages. And before long, large-scale population studies of ancient diseases will teach us more about the ways in which human beings and diseases co-exist and interact.

It's too bad that pioneering mummy scientist Aidan Cockburn isn't alive to witness the recent progress in the field he did so much to advance. He dreamed that mummy science would lead us to better understand how diseases evolve, why and when epidemics occur, and how the rise and fall of certain diseases connect to human evolution. Until recently, paleopathology had to limit itself to the study of specific diseases in ancient individuals. Now it can begin to look at how diseases have interacted with human communities over time, potentially as far back as the early stages of human evolution. One of the payoffs from such work will likely be the calibration of the molecular clock so that we can pinpoint much more precisely when different stages of evolution occurred.

Such broad-based studies will be immensely enhanced by the expanding store of ancient tissue available for researchers. Long after the Manchester Mummy Tissue Bank has reached its limit at somewhere between one and two thousand deposits from different mummies outside Egypt, archeologists will be digging up new mummies from the Valley of the Nile. As Rosalie David puts it, "the potential supply of Egyptian mummies is virtually inexhaustible."

At least as interesting as the diseases we have found in ancient Egyptians are the diseases we haven't found, diseases that belong to our time, not theirs. As yet, there is relatively little evidence of cancer in Egyptian remains — although the Dakleh Oasis Project, a Canadian-led study of an ancient community in Egypt's western desert, has found a possible case of ancient leukemia. Since most cancers occur in middle age or later, part of the explanation for their rarity in ancient remains may be the simple fact that few Egyptians lived long enough to develop them.

As mummy science evolves, it will undoubtedly feed the work of contemporary forensic pathologists. Perhaps techniques for the rebuilding of mummy DNA will aid in the identification of badly decayed bodies of crime victims.

No ONE CAN PREDICT WHERE THE STUDY OF ANCIENT REMAINS WILL LEAD. BUT THE FIELD OF paleopathology now encompasses research on mummies from many parts of the world. Dr. Arthur Aufderheide, an American specialist in South American mummies, and his Colombian colleague, Dr. Felipe Ghul, have recently used DNA techniques to develop a method of identifying the parasite that causes Chagas disease, an ailment confined mostly to Central and South America, that is transmitted by an insect called either the assassin bug or the kissing bug. They plan to use this technique to launch a major study of Chagas disease in tissue from Andean mummies. Unquestionably, the areas opened up by DNA study will continue to be the most exciting. But mummy tissue may give up all sorts of other secrets. For example, did the Egyptians use mind-altering drugs?

In Manchester, tissue from the Mummy Tissue Bank is now contributing to a major study of drug use in ancient Egypt. Traces of cannabis have been found in some mummy tissue. Given that the Egyptians grew hemp, this result is hardly surprising. Recently, however, a German researcher claimed to have found evidence of cocaine and nicotine. Since both derive from plants originating in South America, this would be sensational news indeed, indicating contact between the ancient Egyptians and pre-Columbian peoples. But in a parallel study, when samples of tissue from other mummies were examined by members of the Manchester Mummy Research Project, neither substance could be found.

Did the Egyptians value the blue lotus (above) for its beauty and its perfume or for its hallucinogenic powers? Mummy science may someday soon solve this riddle.

One of the most intriguing questions about drug use surrounds the blue lotus, a flower frequently depicted in Egyptian wall paintings of feasts and celebrations. Revelers are often shown sniffing bowls of wine in which blue lotuses are floating. Were these flowers merely decorative or were they also hallucinogens, as some have speculated? At least one mummy was found buried on a bed of blue lotus blossoms, perhaps indicating that the flower was believed to have special pleasure-giving properties.

These and countless other conversations with mummies will continue to expand our knowledge of the past, bringing us ever closer to the ancient Egyptian world. The more we learn about these fascinating ancestors, the more familiar they become. We can imagine their joys and triumphs, their cares and concerns. If mummy science has taught us anything, it is that these were not mythic, godlike beings but flesh-and-blood people.

In another sense, however, the more we know about the people who lived in the land of the pharaohs, the further away they seem. The gaps in our knowledge loom even wider, the enigmas vex us even more. In recent years, we have added many words to our ancient Egyptian vocabulary, but the lexicon will always be incomplete. We will never be able to fill in all the missing vowels. In the end, we will be left with the same contradiction one feels when first standing before the unwrapped form of a person buried three thousand years ago. Lying before us is a body, shrunken and decayed by time and disease, who is nevertheless a recognizable individual. Suddenly our nostrils fill with a delicious spicy scent. The scent is at once familiar and impossibly remote. Like the ancient Egyptians themselves.

TIMELINE
HIGHLIGHTS OF ANCIENT EGYPTIAN CHRONOLGY

PREDYNASTIC PERIOD
(CA. 5000-3100 B.C.E)

ARCHAIC PERIOD
(CA. 3100-2686 B.C.E.)

- *Dynasty 1 (ca. 3100-2890)*

| ca. 3100 | Menes |
| ca. 2985-2930 | Den |

- *Dynasty 2 (ca. 2890-2686)*

| ca. 2700 | Peribsen |

OLD KINGDOM
(CA. 2686-CA. 2181 B.C.E.)

- *Dynasty 3 (ca. 2686-2613)*

| ca. 2667-2648 | Djoser |

- *Dynasty 4 (ca. 2613-2494)*

ca. 2613-2589	Sneferu
ca. 2589-2566	Cheops
ca. 2558-2533	Chephren
ca. 2528-2500	Mycerinus
ca. 2500-2496	Shepseskaf

- *Dynasty 5 (ca. 2494-2345)*

ca. 2494-2487	Userkaf
ca. 2487-2473	Sahure
ca. 2473-2463	Neferirkare (Kakai)
ca. 2463-2422	Niuserre
ca. 2375-2345	Unas

- *Dynasty 6 (ca. 2345-2181)*

ca. 2345-2333	Teti
ca. 2322-2283	Pepy I
2269-ca. 2175	Pepy II

FIRST INTERMEDIATE PERIOD
(CA. 2181-1991 B.C.E.)

- *Dynasty 7 (ca. 2181-2173)*
  Memphis-based rulers

- *Dynasty 8 (ca. 2173-2160)*
  Memphis-based rulers

- *Dynasty 9 (ca. 2160-2130)*

| ca. 2160 | Achthoes I |
| | Heracleopolis-based rulers |

- *Dynasty 10 (ca. 2130-2040)*
  Heracleopolis-based rulers

- *Dynasty 11 (ca. 2133-1991)*

2060-2010	Nebhepetre
2009-1998	S'ankhkare
1997-1991	Nebtowyre

MIDDLE KINGDOM
(1991-1786 B.C.E.)

- *Dynasty 12 (1991-1786)*

1991-1962	Amenemhet I
1971-1928	Senusret I
1929-1895	Amenemhet II
1897-1878	Senusret II
1878-1843	Senusret III
1842-1797	Amenemhet III
1798-1790	Amenemhet IV
1789-1786	Queen Sobekneferu

SECOND INTERMEDIATE PERIOD
(1786-1567 B.C.E.)

- *Dynasty 13 (1786-1633)*
  Thebes-based rulers

- *Dynasty 14 (1786-ca. 1603)*
  Xois-based rulers

- *Dynasty 15 (1674-1567)*

| ca. 1570 | Auserre Apophis I |

- *Dynasty 16 (ca. 1684-1567)*

- *Dynasty 17 (ca. 1650-1567)*

| ca. 1575 | Seqenenre Ta'o II |
| ca. 1570-1567 | Kamose |

NEW KINGDOM
(1567-1085 B.C.E.)

- *Dynasty 18 (1567-1320)*

1570-1546	Amosis I
1546-1526	Amenhotep I
1525-1512	Tuthmosis I
ca. 1512-1504	Tuthmosis II
1503-1482	Queen Hatshepsut
1482-1450	Tuthmosis III
1450-1425	Amenhotep II
1425-1417	Tuthmosis IV
1417-1379	Amenhotep III
1379-1362	Amenhotep IV (Akhenaten)
ca. 1364-1361	Smenkhkare
1361-1352	Tutankhamen
1352-1348	Ay
1348-1320	Horemheb

- *Dynasty 19 (1320-1200)*

1318-1304	Sethos I
1304-1237	Ramesses II
1236-1223	Merenptah

- *Dynasty 20 (1200-1085)*

ca.1186-1184	Sethnakhte
1198-1166	Ramesses III
1160-1156	Ramesses V
1140-1121	Ramesses IX
1113-1085	Ramesses XI

THIRD INTERMEDIATE PERIOD (1089-525 B.C.E.)

- *Dynasty 21 (ca. 1089-945)*

Tanis-based kings:

1089-1063	Smendes
1063-1037	Psusennes I
959-945	Psusennes II

Thebes-based high priests:

1100-1094	Herihor
1064-1045	Pinudjem I
985-969	Pinudjem II

- *Dynasty 22 (945-730)*

945-924	Sheshonq I
874-850	Osorkon II

- *Dynasty 23 (ca. 818-793)*

	Tanis-based rule

- *Dynasty 24 (ca. 727-715)*

	Sais-based rule

- *Dynasty 25 (ca. 780-656)*

716-702	Shabako
690-664	Taharka
664-656	Tanuatamun

- *Dynasty 26 (664-525)*

664-610	Psammetichus I
610-595	Necho II
595-589	Psammetichus II
589-570	Apries
570-526	Amasis
526-525	Psammetichus III

LATE PERIOD (525-332 B.C.E.)

First Persian Period

- *Dynasty 27 (525-404)*

525-522	Cambyses
521-486	Darius I

- *Dynasty 28 (404-399)*

	Sais-based rulers

- *Dynasty 29 (399-380)*

	Mendes-based rulers

- *Dynasty 30 (380-343)*

380-363	Nectanebo I

Second Persian Period

- *Dynasty 31 (343-332)*

	Persian kings
332	Conquest of Egypt by Alexander the Great

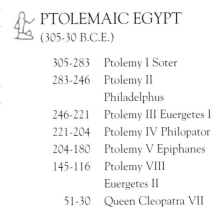

PTOLEMAIC EGYPT (305-30 B.C.E.)

305-283	Ptolemy I Soter
283-246	Ptolemy II Philadelphus
246-221	Ptolemy III Euergetes I
221-204	Ptolemy IV Philopator
204-180	Ptolemy V Epiphanes
145-116	Ptolemy VIII Euergetes II
51-30	Queen Cleopatra VII

ROMAN EGYPT (30 B.C.E.-CA. 600 C.E.)

193 C.E.-211	Septimius Severus
249-251	Decius
284-305	Diocletian
306-337	Constantine I
379-395	Theodosius I
ca. 600 C.E.	Arab conquest of Egypt

ACKNOWLEDGMENTS

I would like to thank the editorial and production team at Madison Press Books for all their advice and support, and in particular Hugh Brewster, who originally suggested the idea for the book; Rick Archbold, whose text so aptly explains and illuminates the scientific studies we pursue in the search to uncover the lives of the ancient Egyptians; and Mireille Majoor, who has taken the book through its various stages of production.

I am grateful to Geoffrey Thompson, Photographer at the University of Manchester, for producing the photographic material relating to the Manchester Museum and the Manchester Mummy Research Project.

I should like to pay tribute to the work of all my colleagues who have been part of the Manchester Egyptian Mummy Project for the past 27 years; it has been our good fortune to share the excitement of helping to develop the scientific study of Egyptian mummies.

— *Rosalie David*

The writing of *Conversations with Mummies* brought me into contact with a fascinating group of pioneers in the field of paleopathology on both sides of the Atlantic and with a number of specialists in Egyptology. Without the help of these experts, this book would not have been possible.

For me, this book began with a visit to Manchester in June of 1999, where I first met Rosalie David and was introduced to her fascinating work. She has been a wonderful collaborator, whose knowledge of Egypt, Egyptology, and paleopathology continues to amaze. Several of Rosalie's Manchester Mummy Project colleagues willingly provided their memories and insights: Patricia Lambert-Zazulak, Patricia Rutherford, Dr. Edmund Tapp, and Ken Wildsmith. Special thanks to Tricia Rutherford for the time she spent patiently explaining the complex task of preparing ancient tissue for microscopic analysis.

I was lucky to meet several of those involved in the North American mummy autopsies of the early 1970s, either by phone or in person. They talked to me at length and looked over parts of the manuscript: Eve Cockburn, Gerald Hart, Patrick Horne, Peter Lewin, Nicholas Millet, and Theodore Reyman.

Several people helped me gain access to rare video footage of the early autopsies: John Waters of Detroit, Kathryn Rumboldt of Toronto's University Health Network, and Michelle Milady of CBC television.

Dr. Stephen Quirke of London's Petrie Museum of Egyptian Archaeology showed me the collection and gave me access to its photo archives.

Stephanie Holowka of Toronto's Hospital for Sick Children made sure I understood the ins and outs of Djedmaatesankh's CAT scan and its subsequent computer analysis. Bob Brier took the time to talk to me about his modern re-enactment of ancient Egyptian mummification. Arthur Aufderheide gave me a marvelous overview of the current field of paleopathology. Gayle Gibson of the Royal Ontario Museum's Education Department brought Djedmaatesankh back to life and deciphered the fine points of her coffin. Rosemary Hillary transcribed my taped interviews with her usual speed, accuracy, and good humor.

Toronto Egyptologist Peter Brand read every word of the text more than once and saved me from many errors. His extraordinary expertise made a difference on almost every page and in almost every caption.

A special note of thanks to two of those already mentioned above. Peter Lewin gave freely of his time and his wide experience of paleopathology and lent me mountains of material from his personal files and his personal library. Patrick Horne not only offered his recollections and opened up his comprehensive library of books on mummies and mummy science, he made sure I understood the crucial and all-too-often-overlooked work of laboratory technologists.

Lastly, kudos to the editorial and production team at Madison Press — Hugh Brewster, Susan Aihoshi, Sandra Hall, Cathy Fraccaro, Imoinda Romain, and Joanne Chow — but especially to the world's only living *ushabti*, Mireille Majoor, whose editorial acumen and unflagging dedication to this project will surely guarantee her a positive verdict at the judgment of truth. We've been on many interesting voyages together, but this has been one of the most memorable. Finally, a salute to copy editor Kathryn Dean and her undying quest for prose perfection.

— *Rick Archbold*

CREDITS

Every effort has been made to correctly attribute all material reproduced in this book. If errors have unwittingly occurred, we will be happy to correct them in future editions.

Front cover: Scala/Art Resource
Front flap: Photograph courtesy of Royal Ontario Museum © ROM
Back flap: Art Resource/Erich Lessing
Back cover: (Left) Ancient Art and Architecture Collection, (right) Photograph courtesy of Royal Ontario Museum © ROM, (bottom) Griffith Institute, Ashmolean Museum
Endpapers: The Art Archive/ British Museum
1: AKG London/Erich Lessing
2-3: Bridgeman Art Library/Stapleton Collection, UK
4: The Art Archive/Egyptian Museum, Cairo
6-7: Robert Harding Picture Library/© Nigel Francis
8-9: Kenneth Garrett/NGS Image Collection
11: The Art Archive/Egyptian Museum, Cairo
13: (All) The Manchester Museum, The University of Manchester, England
15: (All) The Manchester Museum, The University of Manchester, England
17: (All) The Manchester Museum, The University of Manchester, England
18: The Manchester Museum, The University of Manchester, England
19: The Manchester Museum, The University of Manchester, England
21: (All) The Manchester Museum, The University of Manchester, England
23: The Manchester Museum, The University of Manchester, England
26: (Left) Dr. S. Edwards, The Manchester Museum, The University of Manchester, England, (right) KIT, Amsterdam
28: Dr. Rosalie David
30, 31: AKG London/François Guénet
32: (Left) © Corbis/Bettmann, (right) Art Resource
33: The Ancient Art and Architecture Collection

34: Richard Neave, Unit for Art in Medicine, The University of Manchester, England
36: The Manchester Museum, The University of Manchester, England
37: (All) The Manchester Museum, The University of Manchester, England
38: The Manchester Museum, The University of Manchester, England
39: The Manchester Museum, The University of Manchester, England
41: AKG London
42: Corbis/Bettmann
43: Mary Evans Picture Library
44: (Top) Corbis/© Hulton-Deutsch Collection, (bottom left) © Corbis, (bottom right) © North Wind Picture Archives
45: (Left) Mary Evans Picture Library, (right) Robert Harding Picture Library/© British Museum
46: (Left) North Wind Picture Archives, (right) Bristol Museums and Art Gallery
49: Mary Evans Picture Library
50: Corbis/© Hulton-Deutsch Collection
51: (All) Private Collection
52: Reuters/Corbis-Bettmann
53: The Art Archive
55: Corbis
56: Robert Harding Picture Library
57: (Top, bottom left) Griffith Institute, Ashmolean Museum, (bottom right) Robert Harding Picture Library/George Rainbird
58: Griffith Institute, Ashmolean Museum
59: (Top) AKG London, (bottom) Griffith Institute, Ashmolean Museum
60: © The Petrie Museum of Egyptian Archaeology, University College London
62: Corbis/© Underwood and Underwood
63: © The Petrie Museum of Egyptian Archaeology, University College London
64: AKG London
65: The Ancient Art and Architecture Collection
66: The Ancient Art and Architecture Collection
67: (Left) Art Resource/Werner Forman Archive, (right) Art Resource/Werner Forman Archive, Museés Royaux du Cinquantenaire, Brussels

68: Mary Evans Picture Library
69: The Art Archive/Egyptian Museum, Cairo
70: (Top) AKG London, (bottom) Art Resource/© Erich Lessing
71: The Art Archive/Archaeological Museum, Cairo
72: The Art Archive/British Museum
73: The Ancient Art and Architecture Collection
74: (Top) Art Resource/Erich Lessing (bottom) Bridgeman Art Library/Ashmolean Museum, Oxford, UK
75: Art Resource/Werner Forman Archive, Egyptian Museum, Cairo
76: (Top) Robert Harding Picture Library, (all others) Art Resource/Werner Forman Archive, Egyptian Museum, Cairo
77: Art Resource/© Erich Lessing, Louvre
78, 79: (All) Bridgeman Art Library, (left to right) British Museum, London; Royal Albert Memorial Museum, Exeter; British Museum, London; Bonhams, London; Royal Albert Memorial Museum, Exeter
80: Scala/Art Resource
81: Robert Harding Picture Library/ © British Museum
82: (All) Bridgeman Art Library, (left to right) British Museum, London; Ashmolean Museum, Oxford; Detroit Institute of Arts; Ashmolean Museum, Oxford
83: AKG London
84: Brian Velenchenko © 2000, reprinted with permission of Discover Magazine
85: Pat Remler © 2000, reprinted with permission of Discover Magazine
86, 87: (All) Photos by Pat Remler
88: (All) Detroit Institute of Arts
90: (All) Eve Cockburn
93: Peter Lewin
94: (Top right, bottom) Peter Lewin, (left, top left) Eve Cockburn
96: Photograph courtesy of Royal Ontario Museum
98: Courtesy University Health Network © ROM

187

"To most people there are few ideas more repugnant than that of disturbing the dead. To open graves, to remove all the objects placed there by loving hands, and to unroll and investigate bodies, seems to many minds not merely repulsive but bordering on sacrilege. And yet these same people would not hesitate to wear a scarab-ring taken off a dead man's hand; they willingly buy strings of beads which were found round a mummy's neck; they will handle without qualm amulets that were found actually inside a body. In short they encourage, for their own pleasure and amusement, the rifling of graves for gain by the natives. To such people I have nothing to say. Their objections—their opinions even—are an offence to science. . ."

Margaret Alice Murray in the Introduction to *The Tomb of the Two Brothers,* 1910

SELECTED BIBLIOGRAPHY

This is by no means a comprehensive list of all the books and other sources consulted in the preparation of *Conversations with Mummies*. It is meant to highlight the most useful or the most accessible works for those interested in learning more about ancient Egypt and paleopathology.

Brier, Bob. *Egyptian Mummies: Unraveling the Secrets of an Ancient Art*. New York: William Morrow, 1994.

———. *Encyclopedia of Mummies*. New York: Checkmark Books, 1998.

Bucaille, Maurice. *Mummies of the Pharaohs: Modern Medical Investigations*. New York: St. Martin's Press, 1990.

Carter, Howard. *The Tomb of Tutankhamen*. 1925. Reprint, New York: Cooper Square, 1963.

Ceram, C. W. *Gods, Graves, and Scholars*. 2nd ed. New York: Alfred Knopf, 1967.

———. *The March of Archaeology*. New York: Alfred A. Knopf, 1958.

Cockburn, Aidan, Eve Cockburn, and Theodore A. Reyman, eds. *Mummies, Disease & Ancient Cultures*. 2nd ed. Cambridge: Cambridge University Press, 1998.

Collier, Mark, and Bill Manley. *How to Read Egyptian Hieroglyphs: A Step-by-Step Guide to Teach Yourself*. Berkeley and Los Angeles: University of California Press, 1998.

D'Auria, Sue, et al. *Mummies & Magic: The Funerary Arts in Ancient Egypt*. Boston: Museum of Fine Arts, Boston, 1992 & 1998.

David, A. Rosalie. *The Ancient Egyptians: Beliefs and Practices*. Brighton, England, and Portland, Oregon: Sussex Academic Press, 1998.

———. *Handbook to Life in Ancient Egypt*. New York: Facts on File, 1998.

———. *The Mummy's Tale*. New York: St. Martin's Press, 1993.

———. *The Pyramid Builders of Ancient Egypt: A Modern Investigation of Pharaoh's Workforce*. London and New York: Routledge, 1986.

David, A. Rosalie, ed. *Manchester Museum Mummy Project: Multidisciplinary Research on Ancient Egyptian Mummified Remains*. Manchester: Manchester Museum, 1979.

———. *Mysteries of the Mummies*. London: Cassell, 1978.

———. *Science in Egyptology*. Manchester: Manchester University Press, 1986.

David, A. Rosalie, and Eddie Tapp, eds. *Evidence Embalmed: Modern Medicine and the Mummies of Ancient Egypt*. Manchester: Manchester University Press, 1984.

Drower, Margaret S. *Flinders Petrie: A Life in Archaeology*. London: Gollancz, 1985.

Ghalioungui, Paul. *The House of Life Per Ankh: Magic and Medical Science in Ancient Egypt*. London: Hodder and Stoughton, 1963.

Harris, James E., and Kent R. Weeks. *X-Raying the Pharaohs*. New York: Charles Scribner's Sons, 1973.

Harris, James E., and Edward F. Wente. *An X-Ray Atlas of the Royal Mummies*. Chicago and London: University of Chicago Press, 1980.

Hart, Gerald D., M.D., ed. *Disease in Ancient Man: An International Symposium*. Toronto: Clarke Irwin, 1983.

Ikram, Salim, and Aidan Dodson. *The Mummy in Ancient Egypt: Equipping the Dead for Eternity*. London: Thames and Hudson, 1998.

Katz, Michael, M.D., et al. *Parasitic Diseases*. New York, Heidelberg and Berlin: Springer-Verlag, 1982.

Kitchen, K. A. *Pharaoh Triumphant: The Life and Times of Ramses II*. Warminster, England: Aris & Phillips, 1982.

Lichtheim, Miriam. *Ancient Egyptian Literature*. Vols. 1 & 2. Berkeley, Los Angeles and London: University of California Press, 1973 & 1975.

Lucas, A., and J. R. Harris. *Ancient Egyptian Materials and Industries*. 4th ed. London: Edward Arnold, 1962.

Manniche, Lise. *An Ancient Egyptian Herbal*. London: British Museum Press, 1989.

Murray, Margaret Alice. *My First Hundred Years*. London: William Kimber, 1963.

———. *The Tomb of the Two Brothers*. Manchester: Manchester Museum, 1910.

Nicholson, P. N., and I. Shaw, eds. *Ancient Egyptian Materials and Technology*. Cambridge: Cambridge University Press, 2000.

Nunn, John F. *Ancient Egyptian Medicine*. London: British Museum Press, 1996.

Petrie, W. M. Flinders. *Seventy Years in Archaeology*. New York: Henry Holt, 1932.

Pettigrew, Thomas J. *A History of Egyptian Mummies*. 1834. Reprint, Los Angeles: North American Archives, 1985.

Smith, G. Elliot. *The Royal Mummies*. Cairo: Institut français d'archéologie orientale, 1912.

Smith, G. Elliot, and Warren R. Dawson. *Egyptian Mummies*. London: George Allen & Unwin, 1924.

Strouhal, Eugen. *Life of the Ancient Egyptians*. London: Opus Publishing, 1992.

Taylor, John H. *Unwrapping a Mummy: The Life, Death, and Embalming of Horemkenesi*. London: British Museum Press, 1995.

Vercoutter, Jean. *The Search for Ancient Egypt*. London: Thames and Hudson, 1992.

Weeks, Kent R. *The Lost Tomb*. New York: William Morrow, 1998.

INDEX

Design and Typography

Gordon Sibley Design, Inc.

Editorial Director

Hugh Brewster

Project Editor

Mireille Majoor

Editorial Assistance

Susan Aihoshi

Production Director

Susan Barrable

Production Coordinator

Sandra L. Hall

Color Separation

Colour Technologies

Printing and Binding

Oceanic Graphic Printing

Conversations with Mummies
was produced by Madison Press Books,
which is under the direction of
Albert E. Cummings